ORIGIN
A Genesis Family Devotional

By Stephen R. Clark

Copyright © 2023 Stephen R. Clark

All rights reserved.

ISBN: 978-1-935256-06-9

All Scripture is taken from the NEW AMERICAN STANDARD BIBLE, Copyright 1960, 1062, 1963, 1968, 1971, 1972, 1973, 1975, 1977, 1995 by The Lockman Foundation. Used by permission.

Because of the dynamic nature of the Internet, any web addresses or links contained in this book may have changed since publication and may no longer be valid.

To my fantastic GRANDchildren Charles and Isabelle, the inspiration for and the recipients of these devotions.

An origin story serves both epistemological and ontological functions. It infuses everyday life and relations with significance and explaining why things are as they are and providing guidance for how things should evolve based upon what we already understand about our world.

— Professor Jessica Shelby

Forward

The most fascinating genre of storytelling is the origin story. It reveals how the hero or heroine started their storied life. These revelations are true for both fiction and non-fiction. There is something that draws the heart to know how it all began. But more specifically, how you began. Unlike Spiderman, Batman, or even the Lone Ranger, your origin story eclipses them all. More than likely, you have even invested in attempting to discover your roots. But inevitably, it has led you to destinations in the past that have little to say about you today. Even with sophisticated DNA testing, the only result is some vague location in the world with little context for your current life. Consequently, your origin story remains at some blurred point in the past that has no relationship with the present.

That is why knowing your true origin story is so essential. Understanding your origin gives the basis for your reason for being. It is the reason why an adopted child desires to know their biological parents. Knowing your origins gives you a foundation for understanding who you are. It rewards you with a lens through which you interpret the world. Just think how important your birth is for you. Where and to whom you were born influence every aspect of your life. The name you have, how you speak, relate to others, understand family, and your work ethic pertain directly to your origins. And that only deals with your birth. What if you knew the origin of the entire human race? Why we are all like we are.

Every person on the planet, no matter who they are, has a worldview. A worldview, as the word says, is how a person views the world. Try this yourself. Get a magnifying glass. Without using the magnifying glass, look at the carpet at your feet. Now, using the magnifying glass, look at the same place. The glass makes a difference. The lens of the magnifying glass changes how you see things, just like wearing different glasses. Our worldview is the lens through which we understand the world around us. That means having a correct worldview is of utmost importance.

For followers of Christ, knowing and embracing a Biblical worldview is essential. Likewise, the Scriptures provide His disciples with His worldview. Having Christ's worldview gives each believer purpose. 2 Timothy 3:16-17 says that "All Scripture (the Bible) is inspired by God and profitable for teaching, for reproof, for correction, for training in righteousness; so that the man of God may be adequate, equipped for every good work." These are the very words of God that allow us to be complete and ready for our work in the world.

Three questions work together to determine a person's worldview. 1) What is the truth? 2) How do I know the truth? 3) What is valued by that truth? In answer to the first question, what does Psalm 33:6 say? The truth is that God created everything by the word or breath of His mouth. How do you know that is true? 2 Timothy 3:16 says God inspires the Bible. On the surface, that does not sound too profound. Until you see the meaning of "inspired." The Greek word is *theopneustos* and appears only one time in the Bible. This word comes from two Greek words, *theos*, which is God, and *peno*, which means to breathe. So, the Bible, like all the creation, is God-breathed. The Bible is not just a book but the very words of God. Read 2 Peter 1:20-21.

The third question is, "What is valued by that truth?" Valued here means importance. What does the Bible say is important? The only way you can know is in a disciplined study of God's word. You cannot guess what God considers valuable; you must study. Daily Bible reading and investigation of the word are essential for all disciples. Many critical concepts only come with significant time in studying the text. Remember these steps, "Accurate OBSERVATION leads to correct INTERPRETATION, which allows for positive APPLICATION, resulting in life-changing TRANSFORMATION." Learning the very words of God is crucial to a walk worthy of the Lord.

This devotional guide aims to give each home a vehicle to develop a Biblical Worldview. The design of the devotions is for the leaders of the house to present these concepts as their thoughts. Some days there will be assignments that require a task to perform. Therefore, it involves questioning those participating about what they have read. If there is a feeling that the participants do not understand, the one leading can use the daily articles as a devotion and explain it personally. The prayer is that it will become a valuable tool for instilling the values of a Biblical worldview.

As one who desires to pass on a Godly legacy, you know you can't be there all the time. Therefore, you want to give your participants something that will always be with them, God's word. To do so, set aside time to share one of these daily devotions. During this time, you will read God's word, the Bible, for yourself and those in the home. The object of these lessons is to see the world around you through the lens of the Bible. Start with the beginning of Your Origin Story, Genesis 1:1.

There are six lessons each week of the year, with room for notes at the bottom of each page. The QR codes will direct you to the additional content. Be willing to answer your family's questions.

Week 1, Day 1

In the beginning...

The first word is *beresheet* (the Old Testament's original language is Hebrew), translated into three words in English, "In the beginning." Everything and everyone has a beginning, a place where it all starts. In Genesis 1:1, God begins His account of the world's creation at its inception. Your history has a beginning also. Today your exercise is to tell your origin story, your birth. Make sure you take the time to share the entire set of events.

Week 1, Day 2

In the beginning God…

The second word in the Hebrew Bible is *Elohim*, God. Before creation began, there was God. You call Him eternal because He has always been. Only He has ever existed. It was He who chose to create the world, the universe, and the people. In Hebrew, the name of God is plural, like saying your name with an "s" attached. Using a plural name will give you a key to understanding something extraordinary about God. One of the hardest things to understand is why God would have desired to create the world. The answer is in your desire for family. Today's exercise is to share why you decided to have a family or what is most valuable about being a family.

Week 1, Day 3

In the beginning God created...

There are several things your family can learn from this. Only God created; no one helped Him. He chose to do so, not from necessity but His pleasure. He made all that is from absolutely nothing. Yesterday you learned that before creation, nothing existed but God. God created everything from nothing. Imagine if this was true of everything you needed. You had to create everything from the beginning. Today make something simple such as a picture or a handicraft. While you are creating the item, have the family observe how much had to go into its creation. Do not just focus on the collection of the parts but the production of each component. Discuss how important a plan is to the completion of the task.

Week 1, Day 4

In the beginning God created the heavens...

What did God create? EVERYTHING! The Bible says the heavens and the earth. First, what are the heavens? Just as the name of God, the heavens are always plural. It means there is more than one, yet they are all together. The first heaven is the atmosphere that surrounds the earth. It allows humanity to breathe and live. The second is what you refer to as space. That is where all the planets and solar systems are. Then there is the third heaven. The heaven that you think of when the word is spoken or read. It is the dwelling place of God Himself. There is a great video that you should watch. Louie Giglio, How Great Is Our God.

Week 1, Day 5

In the beginning God created the heavens and the earth.

The second portion of the creation is the earth. Amid the vastness of the universe, God created the world—this fantastic planet. Today, you will show your family something special, the Periodic Table of the Elements. The Table is a list of all the elements that make up the earth. The world and everything on the planet, us included, are comprised of these 118 elements. But God even created these. He then formed them into the world in which you live. Today, look at what God has created and what humans have created today. Discuss it with your family. Which is more beautiful? Buildings or mountains. Paintings or sunsets. Which is more beneficial? Electric lights or the sun. Which is necessary for life? Water or soda.

Week 1, Day 6

The earth was formless and void...

In verse two of Genesis, the Bible says that "the earth was formless and void." What does that mean? You pronounce the two Hebrew words, toe-hoo wa-vo-hoo. Sounds really neat, doesn't it? Say it out loud. The words mean worthless and empty. Together they give the idea of chaos or disorder. Like that closet, garage, or basement you have intended to clean up. All the elements God created out of nothing were swirling around in chaos. What happens when your room is in turmoil? Today your assignment is to help take the disorder out of your house. Straighten up something that is in disorder. Discuss before you start your feelings about the mess. Then when the work is complete, share how it makes everyone feel.

Week 2, Day 1

The earth was formless and void, and darkness was over the surface of the deep…

The dark has always been a bit scary. Why is that? Because you can't see what is around you or what is coming next. The Bible says that "darkness was over the surface of the deep." Everything was in chaos and darkness. Doesn't it sound frightening? It would be if God weren't there. But then it says the Spirit of God was there. Many times, you are afraid when it is dark. But the Lord wants us to know His Spirit is always there. It has been from the beginning. Because you are a follower of Jesus, God's Son, the Spirit is always with you. Even when it is dark, or things are going badly, or you have done something wrong, His Spirit is with you. So today, write out praises that share how happy you are that His Spirit is with us.

Week 2, Day 3

...and the Spirit of God was moving over the surface of the waters."

You remember the first verse of the Bible begins, "In the beginning, God?" The name of God was plural. Future devotions will reveal that God exists in three persons. Theologians call this the Trinity. The Trinity is: God the Father, God the Spirit, and God the Son. God is one yet appears as three at the same time. Hard to imagine, isn't it? God is three distinct entities and yet is one, or the Hebrew word *echad*. Tomorrow you will discover an illustration that will help the family understand. When you get together next, get a candle and some matches. Don't read tomorrow's devotion until you are together.

Week 2, Day 4

...the Spirit of God...

C. S. Lewis gives us this marvelous example. Light the candle. Which comes first, the flame or the light? They arrive simultaneously; light and flame appear in two ways: a flame and a light. Now put your hands close to the flame. What do you feel? Right, heat. When did it happen? At the same time as light and flame. All three exist at the same time. Yet each one is very distinct and has a different purpose. That is a simple explanation of a highly complex issue of the Trinity. In the second verse of Genesis, you see the second person of the Trinity, the Holy Spirit, moving over the deep.

Week 2, Day 5

Then God said...

Verse three is a very, very important verse. Can you see the third person of the Trinity in this verse? Look very closely to see what God is saying. Because you have the New Testament, you can see the third person of the Trinity in this passage. Listen very carefully. Verse three says, "And God said." The verse says God spoke. When someone speaks, what comes out? Words. Now turn in your Bible to another passage. Open it to John 1:1 and read the first three verses. Is that not amazing? It says the Word, Jesus, was with God in the beginning, and all things were created through the Word, Jesus. Jesus is the Word God spoke in creation. He is the third person of the Trinity. Isn't it amazing just what you have learned in only three verses?

Week 2, Day 6

Then God said, "Let there be light."

What were the first words God said? Let there be light. Wow, God brought the light first. There was darkness and chaos, and God made light. What is the first thing you do when you enter a dark space? That's right; you turn on the light. No order can come without first shedding light on the subject. But notice God did not create the source of the light first. He created the light itself. Now consider the true source of light. Go back to John chapter 1 and read verses 4-9. What does it say about Jesus? Make a list of all the things you learn from reading John about the true light. Observing just what the Bible says is your first step in learning how to study your Bible.

Week 3, Day 1

And there was light.

Look in your Bible at Psalm 33:6. What does it say? God spoke, and it was done. Back in Genesis 1:3, you see this happen. God spoke, "Let there be light, and there was light." He said He did. God's work brings us to our first Principle for Living Holy (PLH). The first PLH is Integrity; what you say, you will do. It's more than telling the truth; it is doing what you say you will. When God said, "let there be light," He created light. As His followers, you are to do the same. There was a great young man, full of integrity. His name was Daniel. Read and discuss his story in Daniel 1.

Week 3, Day 2

God saw that the light was good…

Genesis 1:4 begins with, "God saw that the light was good." God's work again brings you to the second PLH, which is Goodness. If you are to live holy as God is holy, everything you do should be good. When you do or make something, you should be able to ask, "Is it good?" The answer should be "Yes." But how do you know what is good? Notice in the text that God determined the light was good. Therefore, it must be that God still determines what is good. Read 1 Timothy 4:4-5 and write down what you see is good and why? You will be surprised.

Week 3, Day 3

...and God separated the darkness from the light.

What happens when you clean up your room and organize things in drawers? It starts as a big pile of things, like toys and clothes. You don't put the toys in the same place you put your clothes. Clothes go on hangers, while toys go in storage boxes. Why? Because they don't go together. One doesn't have anything to do with the other. Remember, in verse two, there was only darkness. Now God has created light. Do these two have anything to do with each other? No, where light exists, there is no darkness. The passage says God separated them. Why is that important? Read these verses: John 1:5, 3:19, 8:12, 12:35, and 12:46. List in your book all the reasons light and darkness don't go together.

Week 3, Day 4

God called the light day, and the darkness He called night.

Do you remember the first time you got something new? Say a new puppy. What was the first thing you did? That's right; you name it. Why? So the puppy has an identity because it can't name itself, and you are its owner. The owner is the only one with authority to give something its name. In verse three, God spoke into existence the light. In verse five, as the owner, He names the light day and the darkness night. God has complete authority to create and to name. As you shall see, He can give that authority to others.

Week 3, Day 5

And there was evening and there was morning…

Verse five of the first chapter of Genesis has something that may seem very strange to you. Can you guess what it is? Read the second sentence. What does it say about morning and evening? Which comes first? Right, it says that evening comes first in the order of the day. That seems very odd to us. You always think of the day beginning with the morning. But God said it was evening and then the morning, and that was day one of creation. Why do you think He put it in this order? That's right; it was because darkness was His first creation. It represents the order of creation. In the Jewish calendar, a day ends and starts with sundown. There is a time when the sun goes behind the horizon that there is still light, what you call twilight (think about our national anthem) and Jewish folks call "iffy." The Rabbis teach that the day ends and night begins when you can see three stars in the sky.

Week 3, Day 6

…one day.

Now take time to review the first day of creation. Get out your Bibles and go through the first five verses of Genesis. In studying your Bible, you must learn to ask these questions - Who? What? When? Where? And How? Who was there before Creation began? From what was the creation made? Where was the Spirit on the first day? What four things came into existence on that first day? What did you learn about who God is? What was named by God on the first day? How did God create? How did He feel about His creation? When did the day start? What two principles for living holy did you learn? How does what you learned from day one affect you?

Week 4, Day 1

Then God said, "Let there be an expanse in the midst of the waters...

Have you ever seen something spectacular and then tried to describe it to someone else? What happens? It is never quite as dramatic to them. Many times, words don't describe it adequately. You end up saying, "You just had to be there." That will happen when you start looking at day two of creation. Read Genesis 1:6. What does God say? Think about what you know from verse two. The earth consisted of what? Waters called the deep. Now, in verse six, you come back to the formless and void waters. God is about to bring order from the chaos. He says, "let there be an expanse."

Week 4, Day 2

…and let it separate the waters from the waters.

You will need a plastic bowl and some cardboard for this lesson. Take the cardboard and cut a circle the same circumference as the bowl. Then divide the cardboard in half. Now half fill the bowl with water. Read this aloud, "God made the expanse and separated the waters which were below the expanse from the waters which were above the expanse, and it was so." Place the two pieces of cardboard side by side upright in the bowl. They should fit exactly against the sides of the bowl. What happens? Now take the two pieces of cardboard, one in each hand, and slide them a few inches up the sides of the bowl. What happens? Compare what you have done with what God said. Share in your book what you have found from your experiment.

Week 4, Day 3

And God called the expanse heaven.

God has divided His creation into two portions, day and night. In verse 8, He names a third part of the creation, the expanse. He could have called it space, or atmosphere, or even the universe. But God gives us a unique name that the Bible uses over 670 times. Just like the name of God, it is a plural noun, heavens. It is plural, meaning that though it is one heaven, it is more than one. Going through the Bible, you will see heaven described in many ways. Turn to 2 Corinthians 12 and read the first four verses. What does Paul say about heaven? What do you think he is revealing? Then, go back to our Genesis passage. What would you name the portion of heaven or expanse that God is speaking of here?

Week 4, Day 4

And there was evening and there was morning,
a second day.

Now the second day is complete. But wait a minute. There is something different about this day. Look at the other six days of creation. (1:4, 10, 12, 18, 21, 25, and 31). What was different about day two? God never said of the expanse, "It was good." Why do you think God doesn't say the expanse was good? When God gives us something you can't understand, does it cause us to doubt? Turn your Bibles to Hebrews 11:1. What do you learn about faith? Now read 1 Timothy 4:4. What does it say?

Week 4, Day 5

Then God said, "Let the waters below the heavens be gathered into one place and let the dry land appear," and it was so.

Today you are going to learn a new Hebrew word, *yabbasha*. It comes from a Hebrew word meaning being ashamed, drying up, or withering like a leaf. You hear it in the saying, "dry up and blow away." But in this form, it means dry land. God now has all the water below the heavens (expanse) to come together, and then what appears? Right, dry ground. Now, what is unusual about that? Get a small container and fill it with dirt. Cover it with water. Let it sit for five minutes. Now pour the water off. What appears? Mud or dry land? But God said in verse nine, let "dry" land appear, and it was so. Read the story in Exodus 14. In verse 29, what did the Israelites walk on? Right, *yabbasha*, dry land. The land was dry as the water receded, just like on the third day of creation.

Week 4, Day 6

God called the dry land earth, and the gathering of the waters He called seas; and God saw that it was good.

In verse ten, God demonstrates his authority over His creation by naming the world's two most recognizable parts, the earth, and the sea. When you see a world map, what do you notice first? It doesn't mean that what you see now is the same as it was in the days of creation. But it is still the same two items: earth, the dry land, and seas, the waters. So now God has named day, night, heaven, earth, and seas. By the way, what does God say about the earth and the seas? But He's not finished with day three yet.

Week 5, Day 1

Then God said, "Let the earth sprout vegetation, plants yielding seed, and fruit trees on the earth...

Do you know how long a fruit tree takes to grow and bear fruit? It takes a minimum of six years to produce fruit from a seedling. Take time to go to an orchard near you. What do you think you would see? Mature trees that bear fruit. You wouldn't even consider how long it took them to develop. It would look like they had always been there. God didn't start everything from seed, waiting for it to grow. Like everything else, He spoke it into existence. It looked like it had always been there on the day it was created. It all came into being in one day. He didn't need the sun to produce light, and He didn't need time to have growth.

Week 5, Day 2

…bearing fruit after their kind with seed in them…

There is a crucial phrase that occurs in verse 11. Before you get together as a family, get as many types of fruit as possible. When you gather, cut the fruit open and find the seeds. (Be sure to eat the fruit) Are all the seeds the same? No, each seed is unique. They are all seeds, but each seed will only produce a tree that will only produce that fruit. What, then, is the purpose of seeds? Is it to produce fruit or trees? The truth is that it is to produce fruit trees. Our God is so great that He made all the vegetation on the earth to reproduce itself forever. A self-reproducing world, just amazing.

Week 5, Day 3

…bearing fruit after their kind with seed in them…

Yesterday you learned of God's unique creation of plants that reproduce themselves. That brings us to our third Principle of Living Holy (PLH). Remember, the first PLH was Integrity; you do what you say. Our words and actions must match. The second was Goodness; you always ask what you have done, "Is it good?" Today you learn to reproduce. Read Matthew 28:18-20. What does Jesus command us to do? Right, make disciples. You are to reproduce "after your kind." As followers of Jesus, you are to share the good news about Jesus and teach others to "observe all that I (Jesus) have commanded you." Christians reproduce Christians, just like the vegetation reproduces itself.

Week 5, Day 4

…and it was so.

Today, you are going to test your powers of observation. Read Genesis 1:7, 9, 11, 15, 24, and 30. What is common to all these passages? "And it was so" is the common phrase for all these verses. God says, and it was so. What does that tell us about our great God? List the things that come from your observations. Be sure and draw on what you have already learned. When you get together, share the lists of observations, and discuss your findings.

Week 5, Day 5

...and it was so.

The phrase "And it was so" tells us that what God had said happened just as He said. This statement says three things about our great God. First, it means He has authority over what He creates. Sometimes you hear people refer to Mother Nature when discussing the weather. But you know that is not true. God has sole authority over ALL His creation. Secondly, it says God is capable. He can do whatever He desires. You call that omnipotence, in other words, all-powerful. The final and most important thing is that because God has all authority to accomplish everything He says and is all-powerful to carry out all His desires, you can trust Him and His word. Whatever God says, He will deliver. You can always trust God's word.

Week 5, Day 6

The earth brought forth vegetation, plants yielding seed after their kind, and trees bearing fruit with seed in them, after their kind; and God saw that it was good.

Look at the last phrase of verse twelve, "And God saw that it (vegetation) was good." God didn't say it was good; He saw it was good. That's a big difference. If someone says that something is good, that is an opinion. Others may see the same thing and have different opinions. For example, one person says that the meal was good, but another person eating the same meal says it was too salty and not good. But God "saw" that the vegetation was good, which means it was naturally good. Vegetation that reproduced itself was good because of its nature. Read 1 Timothy 4:4 and then read Psalm 34:8. What do you think this means?

Week 6, Day 1

...God saw that it was good.

The Old Testament shares with us three names for God. You already discussed His plural name Elohim, which appears in our English Bible as God. It is His honored name, like when people address the President. In our last lesson, you read Psalm 34:8. In that passage; His name is LORD, in all capital letters. This name is Yahweh, which means the "One Who Always Is" and is His proper name. It would be like calling someone by their first name. You will see his name as Lord in other passages. The first letter is capitalized, which is Adonai, like addressing someone by their position, such as the pastor. God is named Elohim 2606 times, Yahweh 6824 times, and Adonai 459 times. Which is His most popular name? Why?

Week 6, Day 2

There was evening and there was morning, a third day.

The first three days of creation end in verse thirteen. Have you ever been to a stage play? What would you find if you arrived at the stage early on the day of the play? You would find a big empty auditorium with seats waiting for the audience, an orchestra pit set up for musicians, and curtains hiding the stage. If you walked back behind the stage curtains, what would you find? You would see high scaffolding with lighting and massive backdrops with their paintings of the play's scenes. Sets and props for presenting the play would be scattered on the stage. Some could be the walls of a house with furniture to give the picture of a home. Maybe stone walls of a castle or even a street scene from history. The only thing missing would be the things that bring it all to life. You would say to one another, "The stage is set for a wonderful story to be told." That's what the first three days of creation did. They set the stage for the most amazing story ever told.

Week 6, Day 3

Then God said, "Let there be lights …

Using the QR code, look at this video, *The Stadium*. What did you see? How did the stadium change? It went from empty to filled. That, in a small way, is what God is beginning to do on day four of the creation. He is starting to fill His creation. Look at Genesis 1:14 and observe, remember who, what, when, where, and how. Who is creating? What was He creating? When was He creating? Where was He creating? How was He creating? God said, "Let there be lights." Look back in verse 3. What had God already created? Is He creating light again? No, the word in verse 14 means "objects that produce light." When you look up in the night sky, what do you see? What do you think the "lights" that God created are?

Week 6, Day 4

…in the expanse of the heavens…

Where did God place the "lights?" Right, in the heavens or the expanse that you learned about earlier. You will discover another step in Bible study in the following few phrases. Earlier in our devotions, you learned the four "W's and an H" questions. Now you are going to add to that the ability to see lists. Lists are essential because they give an expanded definition of God's purposes. In verses 14 and 15, list all God's purposes for the lights He places in the heavens. Here is a hint; look for the words "to" and "for." Then see what follows.

Week 6, Day 5

Let there be lights in the expanse of the heavens…

Take time to watch this Simon Sinek video. What question did the speaker say was most important? That's right; it is the question of "why." Today you need to add to our list the four W's and an H and another W. Like the others, each verse doesn't always have the answer. But when it is, it is crucial because it reveals the purpose of what is happening. Parents will often see a child doing something, and they will ask you, "Why did you do that?" They want to know your purpose in doing what was done. So, when you ask God, "Why did You put lights in the heavens?" What did He say first? Tomorrow you will look at His answer. Today try to remember all the times you hear someone ask, "Why?"

Week 6, Day 6

...to separate the day from the night...

Separation of day and night is the first purpose that God had for the lights He placed in the heavens, which brings us to the fourth Principle of Living Holy, Purpose. Everything God created has a purpose. There are no useless things in God's creation. You may not easily see it, but God's creation has a purpose. The purpose is fundamental in the case of people. God has a particular purpose for each person. No one is useless, and no one is unimportant. Your work is to discover and use that purpose for God's glory. When you think of the future, does it excite you to imagine the great purpose for which God has created you? Remember always that God has a great purpose for you.

Week 7, Day 1

...to separate the day from the night...

How does someone know that a person is in the armed forces? Right, they are in uniform. How do you know which branch of the service they are serving? Because they wear different uniforms. In Genesis 1:14, God set lights in the heavens to "separate" the day from the night. The word "separate" means to make different or distinguish. Just like uniforms displays the difference between branches of the military. Now go back to Genesis 1:5. What does it say about light and dark, day and night? God had already created day and night. He didn't have to put lights in the heavens for Him, but for humanity. He did it for man to see the difference. God always wants you to know the difference. You must realize the difference between light and darkness, good and bad, holy and unholy in what you see in life.

Week 7, Day 2

…and let them be for signs…

Remember when you made a list of the purposes for the lights in the heavens? In the last devotion, you looked at the first purpose, to separate the day from the night. Then God says that the lights are "for signs." When you are riding in the car, you see the signs on the side of the road. What do they tell you? Do they tell you about things that you just passed or things that you are about to see? Right, signs tell you what is coming. God said that some of the lights in the heavens would point to things that are coming. Can you remember a time in the Bible when a light in the heavens told people a unique event was coming? Read Matthew 2:1-12. What did the magi (wise men) see in the east? How important was that moment in history? Read Psalm 8:3-4. You can look at the heavens and know that the God who created them cares for you.

Week 7, Day 3

...for seasons...

Your birthday, Christmas, Easter, Thanksgiving, the day school starts, the first day of summer or winter, are all what? Specific times of the year. You would call appointed times, which is the meaning of the word "seasons" in Genesis 1:14. For example, on the summer solstice, you enjoy the most daylight of the calendar year. On the first day of summer, the sun reaches its most northern point in the sky at noon. Because the earth rotates in orbit around the sun, you divide the constellations (groups of stars) into two groups. Some constellations never rise nor set, and they are called circumpolar. But the rest divide into seasonal constellations. God designed His universe to have its calendar of appointed times. What do you think is the purpose God had for seasons?

Week 7, Day 4

…and for days and for years.

How long have you been here? Are you almost there? How old are you? How long have you lived here? How many days remain in the school year? "For days and for years" is the next purpose of the lights in the heavens. Harvey MacKay once said, "Time is free, but it's priceless. You can't own it, but you can use it. You can't keep it, but you can spend it. Once you've lost it, you can never get it back." God gave His creation this priceless gift to measure the passing of time. The sun and the moon mark the passing of each day. The shadow of the sun indicates the time of the day. The calendar counts years as the time for the earth to travel around the sun. But the calendar that the Jewish people use is based on the moon's phases. Here is an example of the difference. On the Jewish calendar, September 1st, 2018, is Elul 21, 5778. Take time to study how the Jewish Calendar works.

Week 7, Day 5

Then God said, "Let there be lights ...

Something is astonishing in Genesis 1:15-16. Take the time to read it. Now go back and read Genesis 1:3-5. What surprises you about these two passages? Did you notice that by the time you get to the fourth day, God has already created light and separated day from night? What is the purpose of the lights in the heavens? Right, to give light upon the earth. But there was already light upon the earth. There was already day and night. Today you reach something extraordinary in the Bible. It is a day when you don't understand. You always want a neat explanation, but that doesn't always happen. Sometimes you are just left with questions. Tomorrow you will look at possible answers, but today you will dance. That's what the Rabbis do when they don't understand God. Read Isaiah 55:8-9 and celebrate our great God.

Week 7, Day 6

God made two great lights ...

One of the great things about the Bible is that you must consider all of it to understand a part of it. Things that occur in one section have their meaning explained in another area. The Bible was written over 2000 years by more than 40 authors. Yet all of them had one common source, the Holy Spirit of God. Read 2 Peter 1:20-21. Now back to the question from yesterday. How could there be light before the creation of the sun? Read 1 John 1:5. What does it say God is? Now read Revelation 22:5, the last chapter of the Bible. What does that say about God? The light for creation in Genesis 1:3 came from God, not from some created source. Now the light that would illuminate the earth would have the sun as its source. The Bible declares God as the only light source at the beginning and the end. Between these two times, He gives the sun for light.

Week 8, Day 1

…to govern the day…to govern the night…

Do you know some people who live on the earth who have never seen snow? There are people on the planet that have never seen the ocean. But everyone in the world has seen the sun or the moon. Genesis 1:16-18 says that the moon and the sun occupy a unique position in God's creation - they "govern" the day and the night. The word for governing in Hebrew means to rule or have authority. (It also is the word for parable, which leads to a fascinating discussion). You can always tell if someone has authority by seeing what happens when they are absent. For example, if the teacher is not in the classroom, there is no class. If the referee is not present, the game can't start. If there is no air, there is no life, and if the sun were not present, there would be no day. Discuss these statements about authority. Then, fill in the blank: There would be no ____ without the Bible. There would be no ____ without Jesus. There would be no ____ without the Holy Spirit. There would be no ____ without God. There would be no ____ without you.

Week 8, Day 2

…and God saw that it was good.

In Genesis 1:16-18, the Lord reveals the three purposes of the sun and moon. The first was to govern. The second was to give light to the earth. The third is to separate the light from the darkness. In verse 14, you looked at the word separate, which meant to "tell the difference." But at its root, it means to divide. This evening, you are getting dinner ready. Give the one cooking some help. While you are helping, see how often that person "divides" things. Like cutting up vegetables or meat, you will serve. When the knife cuts the item, what happens? It separates the pieces. They are no longer together. You can see the difference but can't join them back together. They now have nothing to do with each other. Read 2 Corinthians 6:14-15. What did you find?

Week 8, Day 3

There was evening and there was morning, a fourth day.

You have reached the end of the fourth day of creation. God saw that what He created was good, and there were evening and morning. There are two words for the places you live - house and home. Remember when you first came into the house you live in now? What did it look like before all your furniture arrived? It was empty, with no place to sit, family pictures, or bed to sleep. It was a house but not a home. But then you put out the furniture, hung the pictures, placed all your items in the rooms, and it became your home. So, God built a house in the first three days of creation, but beginning on the fourth day, He begins to make it home. For what or for whom?

Week 8, Day 4

Then God said…

Before you read the verse this morning, look up the word animate. What does animate mean? Bring to life. That's what God is doing on day five of creation. He is going to bring it to life. The waters will bring forth life, and the air will be filled with life. Suddenly the empty seas will be filled abundantly with sea creatures. The expanse of heavens above the earth will team with flying creatures of every color and shape. Instantaneously, at the voice of God, the void of sea and sky explode with LIFE, abundant life. From a condor to a hummingbird. From a blue whale to a minnow. God spoke them all into being. So many of the Psalms praise God for what He has done. See if you can write a psalm to praise God for creating the creatures of the sky and sea.

Week 8, Day 5

Then God said…

It is time to "observe" the text. Remember the questions: who, what, when, where, and how? Look at verse 20. Who was causing the action? What actions occurred? When did the activity occur? Where did the deed occur? How did the event occur? You will notice in the passage a couple of answers to the questions. When that happens, you begin to make a list. Sometimes the lists can be quite expansive. Other times concise. Remember that not only is every word of the Bible relevant, but so is the order in which it is written. How different would the creation be if birds came forth from the sea and fish filled the sky? Order Matters.

Week 8, Day 6

Let the waters teem...

You now know that the Old Testament was originally written in Hebrew. Hebrew is the language that people speak in Israel. So when you read the words in English in your Bible, it is a translation from Hebrew. This translation presents some problems because each interpretation includes the opinion of the one conducting the analysis. So that is why many great scholars gather to develop what they think is the best translation of the language. But they don't always agree. Take time to go to the website called Bible Gateway. In the search box, type in Genesis 1:20. Then, choose five or six different translations in the Bible box and see this verse's interpretations. What are the differences you noticed?

Week 9, Day 1

…teem with swarms of living creatures…

In Bible Gateway, take a look at a particular translation of the Bible for our verse. It is called The Literal Translation. That means that each Hebrew word is translated into English in the order it is written. It does not attempt to make it understandable in English. The reason is so you can look at the words as they appear. Genesis 1:20, "And God said, Let the waters swarm with swarmers having a soul of life; and let the birds fly over the earth, on the face of the expanse of the heavens." The first phrase is "swarm with swarmers." Sounds funny. It would be like you saying, "run with runners" rather than saying, "race." Why do you think God says it this way? Watch this video, Fish Schools, and see if the phrase could apply.

Week 9, Day 2

…living creatures…

What did you think of "schools" for the phrase "swarms of swarmers." Isn't it unusual that God doesn't call them fish? Why do you think He didn't? Could it be because all sea creatures are not fish? Name things that live in the sea that are not fish. Instead, God says these swarmers have "a soul of life." What do you think that means? The word translated soul is powerful in Hebrew, nephesh. It literally means that which has breath, that which breathes. It is used to represent the entire being of a person or animal and is unique to each. The second word means "to have life." Vegetation created on day three has life (they reproduce after their kind) but no nephesh. The swarmers of the waters have life and a soul.

Week 9, Day 3

...and let the birds fly...

The Bible uses a similar phrase to swarms of swarmers when it states God created flights of fliers. Birds do a lot of things. They build nests, lay eggs, dig up worms, migrate, and even eat from bird feeders on your porch. But what is the one thing for which birds are best known? Flying. Their name is precisely what they do. In the Bible, many people are named for what they do. Read Matthew 1:21. What does it say about Jesus' name? If you did your name, what would your name be? Do you like your name? What would be your family's name?

Week 9, Day 4

...in the open expanse...

When you see someone coming towards you, how do you recognize them? When you look in a mirror, what do you see first? In the past, iPhones used a password or your fingerprint to open your phone. Now with the new iPhones, what part of your body opens your phone? Your face. In the literal translation of verse 20, it says the "face of the expanse." In Hebrew, it is the word *paniym*. It is one of those plural words you saw used for God and heaven. Remember the expanse you learned about on the second day of creation. When you look up, you see the face of the heavens. That is the atmosphere, and it is where the birds fly.

Week 9, Day 5

God created the great monsters...

What if I told you that dragons exist? You would say you are crazy. It would all depend on how you define a dragon. Have you ever heard of the Komodo dragon? You can look them up. What other creatures look like dragons? Right, crocodiles and those Florida favorites, alligators. You don't always refer to them as dragons, but the Hebrew word for crocodile is *tannim*. Why is that important? Because it is the first-named species or kind in the Bible. You saw swarms of swarmers, creatures that fill the seas, and flights of fliers that fill the skies. These are very general categories of animals that would include insects and shellfish. But in verse 21, there is a specific creation of "*Gadol tannim*," great dragons. What do you think that means? Watch this video for some ideas, Dragons. Remember, only God was present in creation. These are just man's ideas based on our limited understanding of God's word.

Week 9, Day 6

After its kind...

Let's just be reminded of the four PLHs you have learned so far. Integrity – Did I do what I said I would do? Goodness – Is what I did good? Reproduce – Do I reproduce after my own kind, believers like myself? Purpose – Am I fulfilling God's purpose in my life? In the third PLH, there is an essential phrase. In the first chapter of Genesis, you read the phrase "after its kind or according to its kind" ten times. Actually, in Hebrew, it is only one word, *meen*. So when the Bible says the living creatures were "after its kind," what do you think that means? Take time to watch this video, After Their Kind.

Week 10, Day 1

After its kind…

When you first started studying creation, you discovered how God brings order out of chaos. As you look at the creation and all the different animals, all the variety of them, you have to see that God likes variety. But all within the order. You see many forms of dogs. Look at the difference, even in your neighborhood dogs. There are all types of dogs, but none look like the others. Think of the difference between a Saint Bernard and a Dachshund. Wow, they are really different. But they are both dogs. All dogs reproduce after their kind, dogs. What are the benefits of variety and order in God's creation? How grateful should you be for the diversity and the orderliness of God's beautiful creation?

Week 10, Day 2

…God saw it was good…

When you are working on something at school, your teacher says, "That's really good." How does that make you feel? When parents tell their children they have done an excellent job, how does it make them feel? Why does it make you feel that way? Because of the person speaking of your work knows the quality of good. They can genuinely judge your work rightly. But it is also because they are in a higher position of authority than you. Is there anything greater than God's sovereignty? As Creator of all things, how much does God know? How necessary is God's approval for you? What does God say about His creation at the end of verse 21?

Week 10, Day 3

God blessed them…

You have probably seen movies where there is a king. When the people approach the king, or the king passes by, what do they do? They kneel. It is a sign of respect and honor for the one with authority to rule. In verse 22, the meaning of the word "blessed" comes from the idea "to kneel." When you were a child, your parents were taller than you. But if they knelt, you would be taller than them. To honor another, you have to lower or humble yourself. How honored or blessed would a person feel if their king knelt before them? Today's verse said that God, creator of the entire universe, "blessed" His creation. The One who brought it from nothing now honors what He created.

Week 10, Day 4

God blessed them...

The picture of God blessing His creation brings you to the fifth Principle of Living Holy (PLH) - Blessing. To represent God in this world, you must reflect His character. The Lord says, "You be holy as I am holy." Just as God blessed the creation, you must also bless those around you. Today think of ways to bless family, friends, teachers, neighbors, staff members at church, a stranger, and the Lord Himself. The question you must ask ourselves daily is, "Have I blessed those around me today?"

Week 10, Day 6

God blessed them…

Take a look at Genesis 1:22-23. Observe the text by answering some questions. Who? God. What? He blessed them. (Swarmers and Fliers). When? On the fifth day. Where? Seas and earth. How? Be fruitful and multiply. Have you ever heard the question, "Which came first, the chicken or the egg?" When God spoke these words of blessing, did He say it to fully grown creatures or those unborn, like in an egg? Instead, he talked to animals who were swarming and flying. So the answer as to which came first is – the chicken.

Week 11, Day 1

Be fruitful and multiply, and fill the waters in the seas, and let the birds multiply on the earth.

Why? The one question every person has in almost every situation. If you are ever around children, you hear it constantly. A wise man once said, "Everyone who knows HOW, works for someone who knows WHY." When you learn why something happens, it gives you purpose. It gives you confidence that you understand your role in whatever you are to accomplish. God told the swarmers and fliers to be fruitful and multiply. He said to have little swarmers and fliers. Then on top of that, have many, many, many. Why? That they would fill the seas and the earth. God desired that His creation be full of life. There was no limit on their number. There never needs to be concern about having too many. The seas and the sky will never be too full.

Week 11, Day 2

There was evening and there was morning...

When you have learned something, you can tend to be ready to move on to the next thing. But you don't want to move by day five so quickly. Today is review time. Gather the family together and watch these videos, Days of Creation. Maybe you have heard of the Ark Encounter in Kentucky. The folks who created that project created these films. A family trip there would enhance your understanding of the creation story. After watching the videos, discuss what you see as really important on the fifth day of creation.

Week 11, Day 3

…a fifth day.

There are massive and vital days that will come into your life. Those days mark events that will forever change your life. Like the day you accepted Jesus as Lord. Your baptism. Graduation from school or college. Your wedding day. The day you hold your child in your arms for the first time. The day God calls you to what you will do for Him. In the creation of the world, you have arrived on THAT day. Of all the days of creation, this one is the moment you have been waiting for. Before you begin, you need to review what has happened up to this point. Timelines are great ways to display events. Get together with the family and see if you can create a timeline of the five days of creation.

Week 11, Day 4

Then God said...

Can you imagine the creation at this point? The seas are full of great varieties of swarmers, and the expanse is full of a vast assortment of fliers. But what is empty of "souls of life" that are living, breathing creatures? That's right, the land, the earth. The dry land is devoid of life. But that's about to change in a big way. Now is an excellent time for you to make a list. Look in verse 24. God speaks into existence living creatures that reproduce after their own kind. The Bible lists three types of creatures. Make three columns on a piece of paper—at the top of the page, list the three types; cattle, creeping, and beasts. Now think of all the land animals you can. List them under which type you think they are.

Week 11, Day 5

Let the earth bring forth living creatures...

So how did you do with the three kinds of God's creation of living souls? Look at the different types of land animals in verse 24. First, there are cattle. You can think of those as being domesticated animals. Animals that you would find today as those animals that people can, to a great extent, control. But then there are beasts. These would be the wild beasts that man cannot tame. And finally, the crawling animals. Animals such as snakes and worms. Now, of course, you can't know precisely what all these animals were like, but one thing is certain - God is creative and likes variety in His creation. So you have swarmers, fliers, cattle, creeping things, and beasts. Wow! Just think of how many different kinds of living things are on earth.

Week 11, Day 6

...and it was so.

Creativity is using the imagination or original ideas, especially in producing artistic works. God displays creativity in everything He does. Look at the variety, innovation, imagination, and originality in all He places in His creation. That brings us to our sixth Principle of Living Holy - Creativity. You are very much in the character of God when you are creative. Making something new, creating something different, solving problems in a new way, or even inventing something no one has ever considered. The key to these all being in the picture of God is in the second PLH — Goodness. Is what you have created good? God gives us the power of creativity and desires us to use it for His purposes. Today create something new. It can be a picture, writing, or an invention. Be as creative as you like and then stand back, look upon it, and see "it was good."

Week 12, Day 1

God made the beasts of the earth…

Do you remember the observation questions you ask of the Bible? Who, what, when, where, and how? Look at verse 24 and answer this question, "From where did the creatures God created come? The swarmers and fliers appeared at God's word on the fifth day. But on the sixth day, God said, "Let the earth bring forth living creatures." Unlike the swarmers and fliers, the land animals were created from the earth. All of this will become important later in your study. But remember this all creation comes by the word of God; the method He uses varies. This approach is present in our lives. God's word is correct for everyone, but He applies it to each of us differently.

Week 12, Day 2

God made...

Two words are present throughout the creation story - created and made. The term for created is *bara* in Hebrew. It means to bring something new into existence. The word *asah* translated made means to fashion something from what already exists. As a created being, you can do the second but not the first. You can only fashion what has already been created, but only God can truly create. In the creation story, God does both, but it is interesting to see when the words occur. Look through our verses and mark those two words. What do you find?

Week 12, Day 3

God created…God made…

Twice in the verses you have already read, you saw that God created. You know God is the only one who can truly create something new. What does the Bible say He created? "The heavens and the earth" and "swarmers and fliers." Now look and see what God made. He made the expanse, the two great lights, the stars and beasts, cattle, and creeping things. The things made were from things that already existed, but the items created were from something that had never existed before. Two initial creations spawned it all, light and life. The light started the creation, and life animated the creation. Up to this point, all that exists comes from light and life. Read John 1:1-10. What do you think?

Week 12, Day 4

Then God said…

And just when you thought everything else was "made," God "created" something unique, new, unlike anything else – Man. Don't you love to go to the zoo? Seeing all the animals from around the world is just so amazing. Is the zoo for animals or people? Indeed, it gives animals a place to live and protects endangered species, but what is its real purpose? For people to see the animals. Zoos are created for people. God had created an entire universe, a marvelous menagerie, but for who? Himself? God is about to reveal the real purpose of His creation – Mankind. Humanity is not a swarmer, not a flier, not cattle, or a creeper, not even a beast. God created all this for His most incredible creation. Ecclesiastes 3:11 says of God, "He has made everything appropriate in its time. He has also set eternity in their heart, yet so that <u>man</u> will not find out the work which God has done from the beginning even to the end."

Week 12, Day 5

Then God said…

Fifteen times the Bible says, "Then God said." Nine of the fifteen times are in the first chapter of Genesis. Today, list what follows in each of the verses using this phrase. First, make sure you record what day of creation it occurred. Then, using your creativity, design a way to remember what God did each day. Once you have it created, take a look and another idea.

Finger Creation

Week 12, Day 6

Let the earth...

You have now arrived at the sixth day of creation. Ask your six observation questions as you start to look at the verse. (Who? What? When? Where? How? and Why?) Remember, you may not get all the questions answered in each verse, but be patient. The truth will come. Genesis 1:24. Then God said, "Let the earth bring forth living creatures after their kind: cattle and creeping things and beasts of the earth after their kind," and it was so. Who? God. What? Said. Have you seen this before? Psalm 33:6 "By the word of the LORD the heavens were made, And by the breath of His mouth all their host." God speaks, and it happens. Why do you think what God says is so very important? Look up 2 Timothy 3:16-17.

Week 13, Day 1

Let the earth bring forth…

God has spoken to the earth and told it to bring forth three distinct types of living creatures, *behemah* (domesticated animals), *remes* (animals that crawl or glide quickly), and *chayyah* (non-domesticated animals). Here is an interesting note. It is generally believed that man tamed animals, but according to the Scriptures, God created domesticated animals before man was on the scene. God was preparing for the coming of man. Notice that in these two verses, the phrase "after their own kind." How important is something if it is mentioned four times in two sentences? So what should you expect to see in the world? Exactly, animals that reproduce animals like themselves. And God saw it was good.

Week 13, Day 2

...after their kind...

Have you ever planted a garden? In that garden, have you planted some of the same types of plants? When they were grown, did they all look alike? Yes, but not exactly. They reproduced after their own kind, but there was some variety. They were the same but different. It is the same with people. They are all people, yet every one is unique. Isn't it amazing? Consider identical twins. They are identical even to their DNA, but are they the same? You can begin to think that if everything reproduces after its own kind, they would be identical, but they are not. This difference brings us to our seventh Principle of Living Holy, diversity in unity. Take time to listen to this video.

Week 13, Day 3

...and God saw that it was good.

Based on what you have seen in creation, do you think God likes variety? He desires everything to have its distinct characteristics. Uniqueness, diversity, and variety are all hallmarks of His creation. On the other hand, everything is unified. It all works together to make the creation. Everything connects for the benefit of all. Each part of the creation contributes uniqueness to one fantastic nature. This truth, you will repeatedly see in the Bible and life. You need to ask yourself, "Is what I am doing bringing together diverse things to create unity for the benefit of all?"

Week 13, Day 4

Then God said, "Let Us …

The time has come. God has spoken into existence all creation except one. Verse twenty-six arrives like the unique event that it is. God has prepared His creation; everything is ready, all the pieces are in place, and all actions necessary have been completed. Now He brings forth that for which creation is specifically designed. He speaks, and all creation holds its breath for what will come. And God said, "Let Us." What! Us! From where did that come? All along you may have assumed it has been God saying things, but no others were listening. You imagine God alone speaking the creation into existence, but no others participating. What does the text say? In our second lesson on Genesis, you learned that the word for God is not singular but plural. Then you realized that God's Spirit was present as it moved upon the deep. But was there another? Read John 1:1-3 and Colossians 1:15-17. Who are the Us that God addresses?

Week 13, Day 5

Then God said, "Let Us ...

Now you see how appropriate it is that John calls Jesus the Word. Jesus is the very Word of God that spoke all things into existence. So how can God, alone before creation, say, "Let Us"? It is all in His plural name. A word in English that is like this is deer. If it is one, you say deer. If it is many, you say deer. So it is with the word for God in Hebrew, Elohim. God is one, and yet God is more than one. You have seen in this first chapter of the Bible God the Creator, God the Spirit, and now because of what John and Paul teach us, God the Son. Since the first verse told us that God (Elohim) before anything was created, you know that Creator, Spirit, and Son were all one in the beginning. This concept is so important to believers. God, in three Persons, had always existed, even when there was no creation.

Week 13, Day 6

...make man...

What would be the difference in saying, "Let us make fish, or let us make a fish, or let us make the fish?" It goes from general to specific. You would say the first is the family of animals known as fish. The second would be a particular fish species, such as bass or trout. The final one would be the fish you just caught. So the same word can mean multiple ideas about the same subject, fish. Why is that important? Because God said, "Let Us make man." Can you guess what word translates as man in Hebrew? Adam! So how is it used here? God is using it to mean all the family of man or mankind. But in the very next verse, the Bible says God created "the man." Not mankind, or even a man, but the man, *Adam*.

Week 14, Day 1

...in Our image...

Before you start, get out a pencil and paper. Draw three pictures. First, sketch a picture of a house. Secondly, design a picture of a car. And thirdly, draw a picture of a dog. Just a quick sketch, nothing fancy. So how did you do? Ask some questions about the pictures. Which of your drawings was of a house, tree, or animal you have seen? Which ones of your images were something you made up in your mind? Who owns the pictures you just drew? How did you decide what your picture should look like? More than likely, you already had an image in mind in all of your drawings. That image gave you a design for what you created. Although it looked like the item you were drawing, it was not the item. Why is that important? "Let Us make man in Our own image."

Week 14, Day 2

…in Our image…

What do you think was the likeness or image of God? Do you think he looked like God, or was God-like in his appearance? Remarkably, the Bible describes what God is like, both in appearance and in attributes. Psalms 104:1-2 says, "Bless the LORD, O my soul! O LORD my God, You are very great; You are clothed with splendor and majesty, covering Yourself with light as with a cloak, stretching out heaven like a tent curtain." The Psalmist says that God is clothed with light. You have seen in the very beginning that God is the source of pure light. Revelation 22:5 says, "And there will no longer be any night; and they will not have need of the light of a lamp nor the light of the sun, because the Lord God will illumine them; and they will reign forever and ever." 1 John 1:5 says, "This is the message you have heard from Him and announce to you, that God is Light, and in Him, there is no darkness at all." If man in his appearance is the image of God, then he too will be clothed in what?

Week 14, Day 3

…in Our image…

One of the blessings of having the Bible, God's Word, is that it is one story. When you find a question in one part many times, you see the answer hiding in another part of the story. What would it have been like to live in the presence of God? If God is light, do those around Him share that same light? Take time to read two passages containing stories of people who were in the very presence of God, Exodus 34:29-35 and Matthew 17:1-8. Who were the two people? What was their appearance? How did the people around them react? The first man, Adam, lived in the presence of God and was enclothed in light.

Week 14, Day 4

...in Our image...

In the creation story, you hear, "God said." Why didn't it say "He thought" or "He decided"? It is because He is a God who communicates. In verse 26, He interacts with the Spirit and the Son. That interaction brings you to the eighth Principle of Living Holy (PLH)–Communication. God has always been communicating with His creation. You have the very words of God in your Bible. Why is that important? His Son tells His followers in Acts 1:8 that they are to be His witnesses. That means you are to communicate with others the gospel message about Jesus. If you are to live holy, you must tell others about Jesus. The question for us each day is, "Have I communicated the truth about the Lord in some way with others today.?" What are some ways you can communicate God's love to others today?

Week 14, Day 5

...according to our likeness...

Image is not just about appearance. It is also about attributes. When you hear the word image, what comes to mind? A photograph, a statue, or some animated android? Do you think of appearance or personality? Does image mean what you see or what you know? Can something be an image but not look anything like the original? What makes the created like the Creator? Read some descriptions of God, and as you do, list what you find. Numbers 14:18, 23:19, Deuteronomy 4:24, 4:31, Psalm 36:7, 84:11, Daniel 9:14, John 4:24, 1Corinthians 1:9, 1John 1:5, 4:8. Based on your observations, what are the characteristics of God?

Week 14, Day 6

...according to our likeness...

How did your list from the passages yesterday describe God? What surprised you most in your search? Do you have a better picture of the image of God? God says He is going to create man in His own image. So what would the man be like? What would be his character, abilities, and thoughts if he were made in the image of God? There are many more questions you could ask. Try over the following days to answer some of them. Fortunately, you have already started this process with your study. God's Word has not been slow in revealing an image of God. Even in these first 25 verses, He has already revealed Himself. You remember the Principles for Living Holy (PLH) Integrity, Goodness, Reproduce, Purpose, Bless, Creative, Diversity in Unity, and Communication. If man is in the image of God, then the same principles should be present in him as in God.

Week 15, Day 1

...according to our likeness...

What does the word integrity mean? The dictionary defines it as the quality of being honest and having strong moral principles. You saw that God did what He said He would do. He was sincere and did not lie. When He said, "Let there be light." What happened? He decided what was right to do; then, He committed to doing something, and then He accomplished the task. Now look back on what was just said. If man is to be in the image of God, then he must be able to freely make decisions, follow them with commitment, and then accomplish what he said. Can people do this? Do people do this? This freedom to decide and then carry out that decision is essential in God's likeness in humankind.

Week 15, Day 2

...according to our likeness...

Which of these things are good and which are bad? Stealing, lying, giving, sharing, revenge, kindness, laughing, singing, dancing, gossiping, worship, friendship, joy, anger, cursing, and blessing. How did you know which ones were good? How did you know which ones were bad? You learned in many verses that "God saw it was good." God could determine the quality of (PLH) goodness in what He saw. That quality must be in the man He created in God's image. It is important to note that the man only needed to know what was good, not bad. How do you think bank tellers are trained to recognize a counterfeit bill? You show them good bills. By making them so familiar with good bills, they would immediately distinguish one that wasn't good. God created man with the ability to recognize what is good.

Week 15, Day 3

...according to our likeness...

Today, read the creation story with this question in mind: "What was unique about all the living things God created?" Did God ever create more of them? No, they all reproduce after their own kind. The uniqueness of all living things God created was that they reproduce themselves. God saw that it was good. So when He makes man in His own image, does He do something different? No, He allows humankind to reproduce God's image in every person that has ever lived on the earth. So all people bear the image of the One who created them. That's why every person on the planet can relate personally to the God who created them.

Week 15, Day 4

...according to our likeness...

Have you ever had someone ask children, "What do you want to be when you grow up?" I bet you've heard it asked on many occasions. What did they say? Why do you think they said that? When they get older, even after working for many years, people will ask them, "What do you want to do with your life?" You have asked yourself that question many times in your life. Why? The fourth PLH is purpose. God had a purpose in all that He created. Mankind, being in the image of God, always desires to have a purpose in life. It is innately in each person. Your desire to know why you are here, what you are to do, seek significance in life, and accomplish all comes from being in the image of the ONE who created you.

Week 15, Day 5

...according to our likeness...

Do you remember what you learned in verse 22 about the word "bless"? It is the fifth attribute of God found in Genesis 1. What did it mean? That's right, "to kneel." It is intended to raise someone up by lowering yourself. Does this mean that if humanity is in God's image, they must have knees? No! If you were going to bless your grandparents, what might you do? You could take a trip to see them. You could FaceTime with them. You could send them a card. What would you have to do then to bless them? You would have to stop doing something for yourself and put your effort into providing what it took to bless them. In other words, you can't think of yourself to bless another. So if humanity is in the image of God, they must have the ability to deny their own need to bless others.

Week 15, Day 6

...according to our likeness...

Get a piece of paper and a writing instrument for each family member. Number your paper from one to four. Here are four unfinished sentences. Have each person write out how they would complete the sentences. 1) I'll never forget the day ..., 2) It would be a good idea if ..., 3) People should start ..., and 4) if I had time, I would ... Now take your answers and share them with the family. Were all the answers the same? Which ones surprised you? Which ones made you think differently? Creativity, the sixth attribute (PLH) of God you observed earlier, turns new and imaginative ideas into reality. If humanity is in the image of God, they must have the ability to be creative. Look for ways to use your creativity today. Don't throw away your answers.

Week 16, Day 1

...according to our likeness...

Because humankind is created in the image of God, they possess the character traits of their Creator. You have begun to explore the quality of creativity. Gather the family's answers to the four questions you responded to in the last devotion. Please take all the answers and combine them into one story. You should include each person's responses. For example, take the question, "I'll never forget the day." Take each of your answers and string them together into one story of an event-filled day. Now add the second, third, and fourth responses. Be creative. It is a little awkward and maybe a little funny. Tomorrow you will see the purpose of this exercise.

Week 16, Day 2

...according to our likeness...

How did you do unifying the phrases? Are you surprised how easy it was to bring unity from various answers? What did you find most attractive in the story you created? What was the most challenging part? Do you remember the seventh PLH? Right, it was diversity in unity. God showed that He loved the variety in His creation. Each and everything He created was unique. But God also showed His desire for unity in that all things worked harmoniously. If humanity were to be in the image of God, He would have to bring unity amid diversity. Name some of the ways you see mankind taking the variety and uniqueness of the creation and bringing about harmony.

Week 16, Day 3

...according to our likeness...

Get together with another person. Your task is to get that person to understand that "God is love." But the catch is you cannot use words. You call the game charades. Now have them choose a phrase and get you to guess. How long did it take? What was the most challenging part? Now select another expression, and this time you can use words. You can't use any words that are in the phrase. How long did it take? Was it easier to use words? How important are words? Who spoke first in the creation story? If humankind is in the image of God, then they must be able to communicate. In the opinion of many, the ability to communicate is humanity's most significant attribute. Imagine what the creation would be like if no one could talk. What hinders communication most? Right, languages. Later on, you will see why that is true.

Week 16, Day 4

...according to our likeness...

Have you ever heard the phrase, "there is too much red tape to get things done"? Or maybe, "that will cost you an arm and a leg." They are known as idioms. Little phrases convey an idea without using direct terms. Red tape means too many things are required for something to get done. And an arm and a leg meant something cost too much. But idioms always have an original meaning. Red tape was used to bind government documents in the 16th century. It was tangled, so it had to be cut to see the information. An arm and a leg referred to portraits done by artists in early America. The painting would cost more if there were arms or legs. So many times, you use phrases without thinking about what they mean. Having studied the meaning of "in the image of God," how differently do you see the significance? Because humanity is in the image of God, how should you treat others? Here are some more meanings of Idioms you might like to know.

Week 16, Day 5

...and let them rule...

Go through your questions: Who? God. What? Said, "Let us make man." When? On the sixth day. Where? The earth. How? In Our image. Why? "and let them rule over the fish of the sea and over the birds of the sky and over the cattle and over all the earth, and over every creeping thing that creeps on the earth." Do you see the importance of observing just what the Bible says? Why did God create a man, according to the verse? To "rule over" the creation. Since this man's purpose in the creation, do you see how important that man be in the image of God?

Week 16, Day 6

...and let them rule...

Some principles help us to understand life. One is the principle of talent, "Talent does not always determine position." Just because you have the ability to do the job doesn't guarantee you get the job. You can be very well qualified, even exceptional at what you do, but the position is not yours until the person in charge says you can have the job. Read Genesis 1:26. What does it tell us about humanity? You know that humankind had the ability by being in the image of God (Integrity, Goodness, Reproduce, Purpose, Bless, Create, Diversity in Unity, and Communicate). But that alone would not allow them to rule over all the creation. That position was given when the sole owner and Creator of all that has been created said, "Let them." God gave authority to man. Not because the man had done something but because of God's desire to do so. In so doing, God limited Himself from being able to do with His creation whatever He wanted. He assured humanity of free will.

Week 17, Day 1

…male and female He created them…

Read Genesis 1:27. What new information does the Bible share in this verse? God created humanity in his image, but what else? "Male and female, He created them." One of the most intriguing things about Hebrew is that there are no vowels. That sounds surprising to you. You are probably thinking, "How do they know how to pronounce words with no vowels?" You might be surprised that you can read English with no vowels. Try this: Tht wld nt b pssbl. Nglsh wrds mst hv vwls. What does it say? Now you write some sentences and let the family see if they can read them. The word in Hebrew for a male is *ZKR*. Interestingly, those same three letters are the Hebrew root word meaning "to remember."

Week 17, Day 2

…male and female He created them.

When you speak about the people who populate the earth, you use mankind. The term "mankind" can be traced back to a specific use of this missing word "mann" from the Anglo-Saxon word "mann-cynn," meaning both a group of men and all humanity. Yet, it is clear from the creation story that God never felt that man was a complete creation. Completion only occurred when the human race God created was both male and female. God, who does everything with a purpose, made sure that you understand that humanity is only complete if it is male and female. Man without woman and woman without man would be incomplete.

Week 17, Day 3

…male and female He created them.

Here's an exercise to try today. Ask one of the family to set up ten items on the table in the dining room. The rest of the family walks in and sees the things. But only as long as it takes to read Genesis 1:27. Then leave the room. Now answer these questions. Name the ten items. Draw the arrangement of the things. Which one is the largest, and which one is the smallest? Which one is the heaviest? Tell why you think the ten items were chosen. List the order in which they were placed on the table. As you went through the questions, I'm just guessing that you were thinking, "How could I know that?" Why would that be? Because you only had so much information. That is like Genesis 1:27. It only gives us a little information about an essential subject. Fortunately, you will have chapter two to fill in the missing data. It's a real blessing that you have the entire word of God.

Week 17, Day 4

God…

You would be surprised how many people who are not followers of Christ read and study the Bible. Every university and college has classes on the Bible. Many are taught by those who do not confess Jesus as Lord. It doesn't seem easy to believe. But it would be best if you remembered different world religions are taught by people who don't believe in them. So the Bible can be read as literature, history, enlightening stories, or just as a book, but not by you who are believers. You know these are the very words of the God who created you. When you came to trust Christ as your Lord and Savior, the Holy Spirit came to dwell in you. The one true God's presence in your life. John 16:13 says, "But when He, the Spirit of truth, comes, He will guide you into all the truth; for He will not speak on His own initiative, but whatever He hears, He will speak; and He will disclose to you what is to come." So each day, when you read God's word, pray that the Holy Spirit guides you in all truth before you start.

Week 17, Day 5

God…

Time for a quiz. Read Genesis 1:28. Remember your observation questions, who, what, when, where, and how? Then, create your own questions to discover the essential facts about this moment. Be like a detective discovering the truth about the case. A famous philosopher named Aristotle said, "Those who wish to succeed must ask the right preliminary questions." Now be sure to write out your questions and the answers you discover. Here is an example, "Who creates the action in the verse? What are the actions of that individual? When does the action take place? Where does the action take place? How is the action taken?" These are just examples. Because you are in the image of God, you can be creative. This exercise is the first step in becoming a self-learner.

Week 17, Day 6

God…

When you go into a room and switch on the light, do you ever think of what goes into allowing that light to shine? It starts with obtaining fuel to power generators, then transmission lines for electricity and distribution cables to your house, wiring to the switch, and, ultimately, the light bulb. So when you open your Bible to Genesis 1:28, how did 1 and 28 get there? Did God give the numbers each time He gave men a verse? No, it is thanks to Stephen Langton and Robert Estienne. Langton was the Archbishop of Canterbury in England from 1208 until he died in 1228. It was he who divided the Bible into chapters that you use today. Estienne lived in Geneva in 1560 when the first mass-produced English Bible, The Geneva Bible, was printed. It was he who provided the verses. So these two men, through countless hours of effort, allow us to turn in the Bible, any Bible in any language anywhere in the world, and all see the same chapter and verse.

Week 18, Day 1

God blessed them...

A covenant is a permanent agreement between two parties to create a special relationship. Marriage is the closest picture you have of the covenant. In the Bible, God makes various covenants with humanity. The first covenant you see in the Bible comes in Genesis 1:28. It is a permanent agreement between God and humanity. Who was present? God and humanity. What happened? God blessed humankind. When did it happen? The sixth day of creation. How did He bless them? With a covenant. Where did it happen? You don't know that yet. Now for the big question, what did the covenant say? 1) Be fruitful and 2) multiply, 3) fill the earth, and 4) subdue it, and 5) rule over the fish of the sea and over the birds of the sky and over every living thing that moves on the earth. God creates humanity and already has a purpose for them. Do you know that God created you for a purpose? Read Psalm 139:13-16. Discovering that purpose involves studying God's word, prayer, and the Holy Spirit's leadership. Pray that the Lord reveals your purpose in the lives of your family.

Week 18, Day 2

God blessed them…

Everybody wants to have a car. There are several ways you can do that. The first way is to buy a car which would make you the owner. You can do anything you want with it. The only person you have to please with its condition is you. Another way is to lease or rent a car. You can do whatever you want. But after a specified period, you must return it in good condition. You never own it, but you have the use of the vehicle. The last way is to have a car supplied by the company for which you work. Many jobs provide a vehicle for you to drive while serving them. You have authority over its use, but the owner provides items needed for operation. To everyone around you, it looks like your own the car. But you are a steward; you manage what someone else owns. Stewardship is what God does for humanity on the sixth day. The Lord gave the authority but not the ownership of the creation He formed. God blesses humankind with the stewardship of all His creation.

Week 18, Day 3

…Be fruitful and multiply, and fill the earth, and subdue it; and rule…

When you do anything in life, there are certain fundamentals. If done well, they are a few principles that will allow things to go as they should. Most of the time, they can be distilled to two points. For example, if you are going to play in a band, the fundamentals are to play the right note at the right time. If you are going to take care of a pet, you must love them and feed them. If you are to be married, the husband must love his wife, and the wife must respect her husband. Jesus said that if you are His disciple, you must love God with all your heart and love your neighbor as yourself. Everything else tends to take care of itself if you do the fundamentals. In God's covenant with humanity, what are the two fundamentals? To fill and rule over the earth.

Week 18, Day 4

...Be fruitful and multiply...

What is the purpose of an apple tree? Bear fruit? No! The purpose of an apple tree is to produce more apple trees. Inside each piece of fruit, you find what? Worms. No seeds. In each seed is the potential not just to produce more fruit but more fruit trees. When God commanded humanity to be fruitful, He wasn't just saying to produce more people but to produce those that could provide more people. It wasn't just a plan to create a single family but an ever-expanding population. That's why he made humankind male and female. It takes both to be fruitful. Each by itself cannot be fruitful and cannot fulfill His plan. God only requires what man can accomplish. By the way, the term "seed" in referring to humanity's fruit will become very important in our future study.

Week 18, Day 5

...Be fruitful and multiply...

If you took one penny and added another each day at the end of the month, how much money would you have? Thirty cents. But if you doubled your pennies each day, how much money would you have by the end of the month? $5,368,709.12. Big difference! That's the difference between addition and multiplication. God didn't command mankind to add but to multiply. The word of God is very exact. It was not God's plan to add to the number of people on the earth but to multiply their number. Read what God promised in Genesis 22:15-18.

Week 18, Day 6

…and fill the earth…

The total land surface area of Earth is about 57,308,738 square miles. Of that, about 24% is mountainous, and about 33% is desert. Subtracting this uninhabitable 57% (32,665,981 mi2) from the total land area leaves 24,642,757 square miles or 15.77 billion acres of habitable land. Divide this figure by the current human population of 7 billion, and you get 2.3 acres per person. If the average family is three people, that would mean each family would have around eight acres on which to live. Pretty impressive. God told humankind to fill the earth. It doesn't appear that after 6000 years of multiplying people, humanity hasn't come close to filling the world.

Week 19, Day 1

...and subdue it...

You may have fish, dogs, or even a cat in your house. Every day you have responsibilities toward them. You must feed them, clean up their messes, and take them outside. If they are sick, you have to take them to the veterinarian. Why? Because you have authority over them. That brings a significant obligation. To care for them properly, you must understand what they need, what gives them the best life, and how best to administer that care. In other words, to rule over them, you must understand them. When God gave humanity the authority to subdue and rule over the creation, He also gave them the requirement to understand how the creation best works. That's why science is so important. Subduing and ruling over does not mean domination, but dominion, the responsibility for the creation's well-being. You must have knowledge, understanding, and wisdom to govern effectively. Where do you get that? Read Proverbs 2:6 and 9:10.

Week 19, Day 2

...and subdue it...

Get your Bible and read two verses written by the wisest man ever. Ecclesiastes 1:13 and 7:25. Why is the knowledge of God's word essential? Why is your education so very crucial? It is the God-given task of humanity so that they might subdue and rule the creation. Solomon says that the task is grievous and afflicted. That doesn't mean it is terrible, but it isn't easy. But the covenant of God requires that if humankind was to do it effectively, they must have wisdom. Now, what about you? What are you doing to acquire wisdom, knowledge, and understanding? If you are to be disciples, all believers are responsible for growth in these areas. List some ways you can do this.

Week 19, Day 3

…and rule over…

First, God said, subdue and understand His creation. Only then would mankind have the ability to rule over living things. Humanity was given the position of rulership, but only where there was understanding. When you see the animals around you in the world, which one's actions can man direct? Can a man make an animal obey his commands? Only if that person knows what the animal needs. If the animal does not need what you are offering, affection or food, it will not obey your commands. The ruling then becomes not dominating but understanding what meets the animal's needs. God created man to rule by meeting the needs of that which He had created. The quality of stewardship is measured by humanity's willingness to understand and provide what creation needs. God mandates the care of the environment and its occupants in His word.

Week 19, Day 4

...over every living thing that moves on the earth...

What part of the creation does God leave out of humanity's stewardship? Nothing! All that is living on the planet is mankind's personal responsibility. God relinquished control but not ownership of the creation. As caretakers of God's creation, how well do you think mankind has handled his rulership? What could humanity do that would improve the stewardship of all living things? Are there areas in your where you could enhance your dominion?

Week 19, Day 5

Then God said,...

Earth is known as the Goldilocks planet. It is just the right size and place in the creation. Take a look at this video, Habitable Earth. Isn't that amazing? Humanity needs nutrients, oxygen, water, and an appropriate atmosphere for survival. If you look through what you have studied so far, you will see God has provided everything for life except one. What is it? Right, nutrients. Humanity needs food. You know, pizza, hamburgers, fries, everything you need to survive. So what does He provide? Read Genesis 1:29-30.

Week 19, Day 6

Then God said, "Behold …

Whenever you finish something impressive or beneficial, you spread your hands around the object to draw everyone's attention and then say, "Ta-dah." Then, like the magician, when the illusion is complete, the ball player that scores, a parent when their child is successful, or when you do something great, you say "Behold." It draws everyone's attention to something significant. You don't want to let this moment go unnoticed. So God says for the first time, of many more times, BEHOLD. What does He want mankind to see? "I have given." God makes sure that He provides for humanity. They did not work to acquire it, but it was a gift. Can you imagine that all the food you would ever need would be provided free of charge? Think of all the suffering in the world because of the lack of food. But in the perfect creation of a God, all was provided.

Week 20, Day 1

...I have given you every plant yielding seed...

Return to Genesis 1:11-13 and read about God's creation on the third day. What does God create on that day? Vegetation and fruit-bearing trees. Now think about what He makes on creation's fifth and sixth days. All the living creatures and mankind. How were the living creatures and humanity going to survive? That's right, and God provided the food through the vegetation and fruit created on the third day before His creation of living creatures. Remember the Principles for Living - Integrity, Goodness, Reproduce, Purpose, Bless, Creative, Diversity in Unity, and Communication. Now add another - Provider. God provides for His creation before the need ever comes. The best provision always comes before the need arises. You have learned the importance of saving money. Why? Because the day will come when an emergency will require you to have money. By saving, you have made provision before you know the need. This beautiful verse tells us that generosity will provide before recognizing the need. Read 2 Corinthians 9:8.

Week 20, Day 2

...it shall be food for you...

So why do you think God gave vegetation and fruit for food instead of meat? There are plenty of animals. Take a look at the creation of the fifth and sixth days. What was unique about animals and humanity? They had the "soul of life," unlike the vegetation and fruit. The creation was filled with living creatures to multiply after their own kind. God designed nothing to die or be killed. God designed the creation to be growing, not dying. It was a self-sufficient creation. That's why the chapter concludes with BEHOLD; it was very good. God's creation did not include death, dying, disease, work, war, hate, evil, greed, or unrighteousness. It was exceedingly good.

Week 20, Day 3

...it was very good...

If you were born around 1950, you received information on world events through newspapers and radio. Later, television added to that. Many things went on that you never heard until much later, if at all. Today things can happen in the most remote places on earth, and in seconds someone with a cell phone has put it on the internet. Instantaneously anyone with a cell phone can know what happened. That is just amazing. But despite that, you meet people daily who are unaware that something significant has happened. That's because everyone isn't listening to the same news source. It would seem impossible that no matter how important the message is, all 7.53 billion people on earth are not listening simultaneously. But on the sixth day, every person on earth heard the voice of the Lord. All humanity listened to the first covenant — "Be fruitful and multiply, and fill the earth, and subdue it; and rule over the fish of the sea and over the birds of the sky and over every living thing that moves on the earth." No one could say, "I didn't know."

Week 20, Day 4

...it was very good...

Did you know that when you see a story with your eyes, you only see half the story? Our senses, sight, smell, hearing, taste, and touch, only perceive half of what is happening around you. An unseen spiritual world exists in the same space as the physical creation. But the most important thing to remember is that it was created too. When you go back to Genesis 0:0, before creation began, there was only one entity, God. Everything that exists, both physical and spiritual, has been created by God. Read Colossians 1:16. The things in the heavens and invisible are just as natural as the creation you see surrounding you. Before you begin the study of Chapter 2, you need to catch up on the hidden side of creation. It will require looking through the Bible for references about the heavenlies and the spiritual world.

Week 20, Day 5

…it was very good…

Suppose you should travel to Giza, Egypt, and arrive at night at your hotel. When you awake in the morning, you will open the curtains, and to your great surprise, you are staring at the pyramids. Yes, the pyramids that had stood for thousands of years. Magnificent shining in the sun. It will be unbelievable. The remembrance of that moment takes your breath away. Let me ask, "Were the pyramids there when you arrived that night? Were they just as real, solid, and massive as they appeared that morning?" Of course, they were. It was just that you couldn't see them. That is how it is with the unseen spirit world created by God. All the places, all the beings, and all the powers are real, affecting your life. But you can't see them. It is like the air. You can't see it but without it; you can't live. As you discover this unseen side of creation, it can be something fearful. But you need not fear because our Lord Jesus is the Lord of all.

Week 20, Day 6

…it was very good…

When you are studying the Bible, you have five questions. Do you remember them? Who? What? When? Where? How? Let's begin with the first question. Who inhabits the spirit world? Read John 4:24. What does Jesus say that God is? That's right, spirit. He does not have a physical form. Three times in John's writings, he tells us that no one has seen God. So, the first person that dwells in the spirit world is God. What is His appearance? One of the ways the Bible describes Him is in Revelation, chapter 4:1-5. Read the description out loud and imagine His appearance. Your third question is when? Forever, all eternity. Now the fourth question is easy; heaven. Not the sky where the stars and moon and all the galaxies are, but the third heaven. Paul tells you in 2 Corinthians 12:2-4. The first heaven is the atmosphere around the earth. The second is what is called outer space. And the third is the invisible spirit world where God the Father lives. Read Isaiah 6:1-4. The whole earth is full of His glory.

Week 21, Day 1

...it was very good...

The second being to dwell in the spirit world is someone that you know very well. He has always existed, even before creation. Turn in your Bibles to Revelation 5. Read it out loud. Can you guess who it might be? It is the answer to every Sunday School question. Right, it's Jesus. Isn't it wonderful to know that our Lord and Savior is honored in heaven for all eternity for what He has done? He sits on the right of the Father in heaven. Who was the lion in The Wind, The Lion, and the Wardrobe? Here He is called the Lion of the tribe of Judah. But that is not the name for which He is honored. What is that name? The Lamb. Why do you think they call Him the Lamb? You are going to find out that something terrible is going to happen to God's perfect creation. The Lamb is going to be the One who changes everything.

Week 21, Day 2

…it was very good…

Remember the devotion from Genesis 1:26 when God says, "Let Us make man." It shared about the Trinity, God, and the Three in One. There was God the Father, God the Son, and God the … ? Right, The Holy Spirit. By the name, you know that the third person is spirit. But where does the Spirit live? In heaven, on earth, in the wind, in the water? 1 Corinthians 3:16 says, "Do you not know that you are a temple of God and that the Spirit of God dwells in you?" That's right; the Holy Spirit lives in you and every other believer. But that's not the only place. Read John 16:6-16. What else is the Spirit doing? The Holy Spirit is in the world, preparing the world for what is to happen. Isn't it a blessing that God has given you His Holy Spirit to guide and direct our lives? It would be best if you carefully honored the Holy Spirit in all of your ways.

Week 21, Day 3

...it was very good...

Search the internet for Valentine's Day. More than likely, you will find pictures of hearts and a strange little baby with a bow and arrow. Have you ever seen a picture like this? What do you call these little children with bows? That's right, cherubs. Read Revelation 4:5-8. Four living creatures! Wow! They sound amazing. Guess what? These are the real cherubs, or as the Bible calls them, *cherubim*. In Hebrew, the letters "im" at the end of a word means it is plural. Can you imagine seeing one? A far cry from the foolish picture you see on Valentine's Day. The prophet Ezekiel in chapter 10, gives a great view of these magnificent creatures that are before the throne of God. Make a list of the characteristics of the cherubim from Ezekiel 10. These are the first of the created spirit world beings. Pretty impressive, and there's more to come.

Week 21, Day 4

...it was very good...

Take time to read Isaiah 6:1-7. This passage introduces you to another created being in the spirit world, the seraph, or seraphim plural. This passage reveals that they, like the cherubim, are closest to God. They glorify Him with constant praise of Holy, Holy, Holy. Why do you think they say it three times? Their description is brief, indicating they have six wings and fly. Their name means "burning ones." Because there are only a few references, little is known about them. But God created them for a purpose. Why do you think God created these magnificent creatures? Take a little time. Read the descriptions of the *cherubim* and *seraphim*. Sketch how you would think they look.

Week 21, Day 5

…it was very good…

Think of spiritual beings. What are the first ones that come to your mind? Angels, of course. There are over 300 references to angels in the Bible. In the Old Testament, the word is *malak*, and in the New Testament, *aggelos*. Both words mean a messenger. God created angels as His messengers to His creation. Why do you think God wanted messengers to His creation? They occupy a critical role. There are many scenes in the Bible where angels interact with people. Read Luke 1:26-38. At times they are referred to as ministering spirits. They must be quite impressive. Each time they appear, they produce fear in the people who see them. Return to Revelation 5:11. How many angels does it say there are? Myriads of myriads mean more than you can number.

Week 21, Day 6

…it was very good…

There are three essential facts you will want to remember about the beings of the spiritual world. First, although they are not created in the image of God, they can make decisions. They can choose. Although they are servants of God, they are not robots. They must choose to serve. Secondly, they play an essential part in the creation story and the story of God's relationship with humankind. They are not just characters to make things interesting. Finally, in Genesis 1:31, on the final day of creation, "God saw all that He had made, and behold, it was very good." The spiritual beings were part of that "very good." God created everything visible and invisible as good.

Week 22, Day 1

Thus the heavens and the earth were completed…

Remember Stephen Langton? He was the one who divided the Bible into chapters. Unfortunately, he missed the boat between chapters one and two of Genesis. Look at verse one of chapter two of Genesis. In Bible study, this is called a "summary statement." It means that it gathers everything that has been said into one sentence. "Thus, the heavens and the earth were completed, and all their hosts." This sentence summarizes all that has gone on in the first chapter. The most important word is completed, *kalah*, in Hebrew. It means to bring to the end, finished. It means that everything that exists was created then from nothing. Our great and awesome God finished, and nothing more has been created. Despite mankind being in the image of God, humanity cannot create something from nothing. Humanity can only utilize what God created many years ago.

Week 22, Day 2

...were completed...

Have you ever worked on a project for school or work that took a long time and a lot of effort to accomplish? When you finished, and it went well, how did you feel? What did you do at the moment you completed the task? Did you start right away on the next project? More likely, you leaned back and expressed relief that it was over. Then you surveyed the project with a satisfying look. Afterward, you just took some time to rest. You know what? That's what God did after the creation. Look at Genesis 2:2. Do you think He was tired? Did the hard work of creating wear Him out? Read Isaiah 40:28. Why do you think He rested?

Week 22, Day 3

…were completed, and all their host.

Go to your closet and get out an article of clothing. Any piece will do. Somewhere on it, there is a tag. It tells you information about who made it. What the fabric is, what size it is, and care instructions. You might have to have a magnifying glass to read it. The care instructions would possibly say to machine wash in cold water, not bleach, and tumble dry. It tells you how to care best for the clothing to make it last the longest. You will find the manufacturer's directions for the best way to care for anything you buy generally written right on the item. Why do they do that? Because the people who made it want you to use it correctly. They want it to last a long time and give you excellent service. Guess what? In Genesis 2:2, God is going to provide you with His care instructions for humanity.

Week 22, Day 4

...God completed His work...

Genesis 2:2 says, "By the seventh day God completed His work which He had done, and He rested on the seventh day from all His work which He had done." Two new words appear in the Bible, work and rest. God describes His efforts in creation as work. That brings us to our tenth Principle of Living Holy (PLH), good works. When God says, "It was very good," it includes His work. Good works are one of the significant characteristics of being created in the image of God. Mankind is capable of doing good works. Read 2 Timothy 2:21. Why does it say you are helpful to the Master (Jesus our Lord)? Anyone can do good things, but only those who are followers of the Lord Jesus can do good works. Good works are those things you do that are in accordance with God's will.

Week 22, Day 5

…He rested on the seventh day…

The second new word is "rest." It is an extraordinary word in Hebrew. It is Shabbat, or Sabbath, in English. The seventh day corresponds to Saturday. What was the name of the first day of creation? Right, Sunday, the first day of the Week. The Bible says that God created good works for six days, and then He *Shabbat*, rested. Earlier in Isaiah 40:28, you found that God does not get tired. Therefore, it wasn't for needed recovery. But there was a need to make sure that humanity required rest. If the Creator of all the universe, who needed no rest, rested, humankind created in His image needs rest. So the care instructions on humanity said, "To maintain proper use of this product (mankind) allow only six days in a row for operation and then must rest for a day." The eleventh Principle of Living Holy is Shabbat, or as you know, Sabbath. A time to rest from labor and to reflect on the goodness of the Creator.

Week 22, Day 6

God blessed the seventh day...

Read Genesis 2:3. God blessed the seventh day and sanctified it, making it holy. Wow, a holy day. The word holy means to set apart for something unique. God did that for the seventh day, Sabbath. Read the Ten Commandments, Exodus 20:8-11. Make a list of all the things these verses say about the Sabbath. Who does it say is supposed to observe or keep the Sabbath? What are they supposed to do on the Sabbath? Did Jesus keep the Sabbath? Next, read Luke 4:16. What does it mean by "as was His custom?" How important do you think the sabbath is for you?

Week 23, Day 1

...and sanctified it...

It is the custom that all Jewish people observe the Sabbath. Now the big question is, do you observe Sabbath? Do you work six days and rest on the seventh? Mark 2:27 tells you that Jesus said to them, "The Sabbath was made for man, and not man for the Sabbath." The Lord informs all humanity that the Sabbath is for man's benefit. When you observe Sabbath (not the day, but the resting), you honor the Lord by worshipping Him and calling all He has done to your memory. But it is also resting that the Lord knows you will need. It is important to remember the proper operating instructions for those made in the image of God. You work six days and rest in the Lord on the seventh.

Week 23, Day 2

This is the account of the heavens and earth when they were created…

Verse three of chapter two ends the story of creation. It has taken many lessons to cover it all. But there are always missing things. Have you ever read a novel or seen a movie and said, "I wish they would have told me more about …" some part of the story? There are always things that you wish you knew more information about. God thought the same thing because He now gives us what Paul Harvey called "The rest of the story." You may not know who Paul Harvey was, so ask someone older. In the following 24 verses, God will go into much greater detail concerning the sixth day of creation. Take time today and go back and read Genesis 1:24-31. Now God will take you deeper into this great day of creation.

Week 23, Day 3

This is the account of the heavens and earth when they were created...

A genealogist is someone who studies the history of families. Because there is a great deal of interest in the history of families, genealogists have created online systems to discover your family tree. You can even have your DNA scanned to learn where your ancestors originated. Genealogy is a history of people. Get your Bible out and turn to Genesis 5. The list is the first history of mankind that God created. Genesis 2:4 says, "This is the account of the heavens and the earth when they were created, in the day that the LORD God made earth and heaven." The word 'account' is genealogy. You are no longer studying the created heavens and earth but the origin of humanity's history. On the sixth day of creation, God created mankind. You are now going to see an in-depth view of how that occurred.

Week 23, Day 4

...in the day that the LORD God...

Have you ever met someone you admired? They may have a significant position, like a government official or someone you have seen on TV or in movies. Maybe it's your Pastor or someone whose book you have read. It's exciting to meet them personally. You feel honored, and at the same time, you are a bit uncomfortable. You address them with their title, "So honored to meet you, Dr. Smith or Governor Johnson." It is all formal, with no real intimacy. But what happens when they say to you, "Call me, Steve." They give you their name and bring about a personal relationship. In Genesis 2:4, God does that. Read the passage for yourself. How is God named? Right, LORD God. No longer just His position as Elohim, Creator. Now He adds the name, LORD. So what is this name? Go to Exodus 3:13-14. Moses speaks to Elohim and asks Him for His name. God says My name is "I AM WHO I AM," which is translated in the Bible as LORD. So for the first time in the creation story, God uses His personal name. Why? Because He will now be in a personal relationship with what He created, man.

Week 23, Day 5

…LORD God made earth and heavens.

When you see a game's announcement to it says, "Minnesota Vikings vs. Tampa Bay Buccaneers," how can you tell where the game will occur? Tampa Bay, because the home team is always listed second. If someone told you a story about going fishing and said, "You were in the boat fishing and got up in the morning and went to get some bait at the store," what would be wrong? Right, the events were out of order. You would have to get up first, then go to the store, then go fishing. Word order is always important. Now read Genesis 2:4. How has the word order changed in this verse? The heavens and earth are reversed to earth and heaven. Why do you think that is important? When you go outside, what part of the creation do you see first? The land, then you look up at the heavens. Up to this point, God has shared the creation story from His perspective, heavens, and earth; now, you will see it from humanity's perspective, earth, and heaven.

Week 23, Day 6

Now no shrub of the field was yet in the earth...

If you looked at the creation at the end of the fifth day, what would they see? Start at Genesis 1:23 and go backward and list every item of the creation. Read Genesis 2:5. What is your first impression of this verse compared to chapter one? Exactly, there is something wrong here! There has to be a mistake. How can there be "no shrub or plant of the field"? There should be plants everywhere. It would appear to be one of those mistakes in the Bible. And think about this; there was no rain on the earth. How in the world could there be all this vegetation with no rainfall? This passage seems to tell us that this story account is out of order. When rabbis, Jewish teachers, cannot understand what the passage means, you know what he does? He dances because he knows God will one day reveal the answer. Why don't you take time right now to dance?

Week 24, Day 1

...and no plant of the field had yet sprouted...

When you study the Bible, you must observe a few principles. One is that context is king. Context is the circumstances that form the setting for an event. You must always take into consideration the circumstances that surround the passage you are considering. Scripture should never be taken out of the context in which it appears. That's why it is so important you understand the culture. Another is that of the infallibility of Scripture. It means there are no Bible errors because "God inspires all scripture." Inspired means "God-breathed." When you run into problems of understanding, like in verse 5, you can be confident that you can find the answers. They will be in the text. So how do you answer this issue raised yesterday? Two parts. Look at Genesis 2:5 and solve this riddle. What type of vegetation requires both people and rain? Does the forest? Do wildflowers? Do ferns? Do fruit trees? None of these require a person to cultivate them. They grow on their own. But crops require rain and man to cultivate to grow in their season. That's why different words appear in 2:5 than in Chapter 1. The terms in verse five refer to cultivated crops, not wild vegetation, what you would call a garden.

Week 24, Day 2

...there was no man to cultivate the ground.

Instead of telling you how there can be vegetation, but no rain, look at a particular word, ground. It first appears in Genesis 1:25. But the importance of the word doesn't reveal itself until Genesis 2:5. The phrase "no man to cultivate the ground" doesn't sound so important in English. But in Hebrew, it becomes quite fascinating. Look at the phrase again. No (Ayin) man (Adam) to cultivate (Abad) the ground (Adamah). Notice anything unusual? Compare the word for man and the word for ground. They look very similar, don't they? Adam and adamah, man and ground. What do you think the connection is? Now, look a little closer at adam. Do you think one came from the other?

Week 24, Day 3

…to cultivate the ground.

Up until this point, God has been responsible for all the events. But verse 2:5 reveals an action that required an entity other than God for completion. The word "cultivate" is first used in this verse and introduces us to the first action humanity would perform on earth. God planned man's work before he came into being. Man would not only subdue and rule but cultivate the ground. One of people's greatest joys is seeing what they plant grow. There is something so exhilarating about seeing the green push through the dark soil. Today take time to plant something. As you progress through your study, it will remind you of man's first physical task.

Week 24, Day 4

But a mist used to rise from the earth and water the whole surface of the ground.

Take time to watch a video about terrariums before reading the devotion. What did you learn today? Pretty impressive. Maybe you would like to make a terrarium. So how does the terrarium water itself? Now read Genesis 2:6. Does it sound the same? There is no rain in the terrarium, yet the plants are watered. Great scientists have attempted many times to explain how the earth was watered without rain. But none of the explanations have held up under scrutiny. The most plausible belief is that the expanse was a vapor canopy that made the earth's environment quite different. But that is only using science to prove the Bible. Here is an essential principle of Bible study. The Bible is the basis of all truth, and all investigations for truth must align with it. You know the Bible is always true, whereas man's reasoning is often not. So you can believe that a mist from the earth watered the land. The terrarium shows us an example of how it was possible.

Week 24, Day 5

Then the LORD God formed man…

Every once in a while, someone does something you have never seen before. Something so spectacular that it seemed impossible for someone to do. Everyone who saw it says, "How did they do that?" You know you just saw it happen for real, but you can't figure out how it happened. No doubt everyone who reads Genesis 1:27 says the same thing about God. "How did He do that?" Read it right now and see if you think the same thing. The answer is in Genesis 2:7. "Then the LORD God formed man of dust from the ground and breathed into his nostrils the breath of life, and man became a living being." This one verse is all the explanation given about the most significant event of all creation. God creates man and only shares one verse about how He made it happen. He spends many chapters explaining to a man how to build the tabernacle, but only one verse on man's creation. Here is a principle to remember. What man sees as impossible, God sees as simple.

Week 24, Day 6

Then the LORD God formed man …

How something starts is always fascinating. Think of all the superhero movies. What's the most exciting story about each one? How they got started. A radioactive spider bit Spider-Man. Superman was sent to earth from Krypton. Iron Man, Wonder Woman, and Batman have origin stories of how it all began. What story would be most important to you? Right, how humanity began, your "origin story." It is pretty short. Just one sentence, but it is overflowing with some fantastic things. Start observing the origin story from the sixth day of God's creation. First who? As you learned earlier, God is not an impersonal God but one known by His name, the Lord God. What? He formed man. Watch this video, The Potter's Wheel. What did the potter do to the clay? He squeezed it into the shape he desired. That is the meaning of the word "formed." Man was molded into what God wanted. No accident, no evolving, no chance, only the purposeful forming by the design of God.

Week 25, Day 1

Then the LORD God formed man…

From what substance do you think the man was formed? Some unique combinations of chemicals found nowhere on earth or metals from outer space. Maybe a magical, supernatural formula of novel materials. Nope, the dust of the earth. Good old mud and clay, like children, play with in the backyard. Wow! How do you know that's true? If you are served supper consisting of ham, green beans, and potatoes, do you all eat the same amount of each? Some will eat more ham, and others will eat more potatoes. All don't have the same meal? Of course, you had the same green beans and potatoes, but in different amounts. Like the meal, if man was made from the earth, you should find the same elements in him as you do in the earth, maybe not in equal amounts, but not something mysterious or not from earth. Guess what? Use the code to look at this graph. They are the same elements, only in different amounts. God formed man, not from nothingness like the creation. He formed him out of the dust of the earth He had already created.

Week 25, Day 2

…breathed into his nostrils the breath of life…

Now comes the unique part of humanity's origin story. God breathed into the nostrils of the man. When do you see someone breathe into another person? When someone is unconscious, you begin CPR. You pump their chest to keep the blood flowing and blow air to get the oxygen flowing in their lungs. You are hoping to bring them back to life. So God formed man, just like you see humanity now. (With a nose and nostrils) And God blows into man's nose His own breath. Job 27:3 says, "For as long as life is in me, And the breath of God is in my nostrils." God blew His breath of life into the man He formed out of the dust of the earth. Very unique breath, the breath of life. What keeps a man alive is breathing oxygen, but what makes man alive is the breath of God. God brought man to life with His own life.

Week 25, Day 3

…breathed into his nostrils the breath of life…

Today watch a fascinating video called Pixar in a Box. Now you see all the countless hours of work and the tremendous number of people it takes to create the films. In that process, they link together still pictures so that they move like they are alive. It is called animation. Taking an inanimate object and making it appear alive. Think about how much time and effort it takes. But are Woody and Buzz alive? Are robots, which are made of inanimate objects, alive? The answer, of course, is no. As creative as he is, man cannot take something inanimate and bring it to life. But God did it with His breath. The passage says that after God breathed into the man's nostrils, the man became a living being. It means that man became one who breathes. Read Job 33:4. That same breath of life in the first man is also in you. In all creation, only man has received the breath of God.

Week 25, Day 4

...breathed into his nostrils the breath of life...

Man is unique in all of creation. You have probably heard someone say, "Humans and animals are the same." You have also heard that humanity is an evolved species of animals. You will find that science today classifies humans as the only extant members of the subtribe Hominina. Together with chimpanzees, gorillas, and orangutans, they are part of the family Hominidae. There are several reasons for this. The first is the genetic similarity between some animals and humans. Another is the physical appearance of some animals and humans. But the primary reason science places humanity as an animal is a need for unbelievers to show creation without God. But the creation of man proves that God created the world. Man is the only being in nature in the image of God. You must understand what is correct and always recognize what is false.

Week 25, Day 5

…and man became a living being.

A phrase should be added to quotes from the Bible, "These are the very words of God." When you read the words in Genesis, they are the very words of the Creator Himself. The beautiful thing about this is that, as you learned earlier, God cannot lie. All the words He says are the absolute truth. So when He describes something, the words God uses are critical. They are not random thoughts getting close to the idea of something; they are specific and correct. Therefore it is of utmost importance that you know exactly what He said. That requires looking at the original language, which is Hebrew. Verse 2:7 describes man as a "living being." In Hebrew, the words are *chay nephesh*. What it says is a living soul. Does that sound familiar? Genesis 1:21 and 1:30 describes all the animals in the same way. Does that mean men and animals are the same? Time to dance!

Week 25, Day 6

...and man became a living being.

What does a living soul mean? All animals, fish, beasts, and birds, were created with two parts, life and soul. Each, when completed, was given a life and a soul. Life is the physical form that every animal has. When the physical form continues to function correctly, the animal lives; thus, all animals live. But there is a second part, a soul. The soul is what makes them distinctive. Take a look at your dogs, cats, and fish. They have unique physical characteristics, but you would never mistake a dog for a fish or a cat for a dog. They all are living. But even among the dogs, there is a more significant distinctive. Dogs each have a distinct personality. Each has a different way of observing the world around them. This is a soul. A soul makes every living being different. But you still say, "Well, man has a physical form, and each man has a distinct personality, so aren't they the same as the animals? Time to dance again!

Week 26, Day 1

...and man became a living being.

You have learned that all animals have a physical form and a soul. You can see it in every animal you observe. But man is different, unique. In whose image was man created? God's. What unusual thing did you learn about God in the very first verse of Genesis? You learned He was plural, one, yet more than one. In Genesis 1:26, you found out that He referred to Us. You learned God exists as the Three in One. What is known as the Trinity. God the Father, God the Son, and God the Holy Spirit. Now, if man is in the image of God, how many parts would he have? Right, three distinctly different roles. You have learned that all animals are binary, with two parts, physical form, and soul. But a man must have three if he is truly in the image of a God. What part is a man missing as a living soul? Now read Genesis 2:7. What did God do when He created man that He did not do when He created the animals? That's right; He breathed into his nostrils the breath of life.

Week 26, Day 2

...and man became a living being.

The breath of life. What does that mean? Read Genesis 7:21-22. What does that verse call the breath in man's nostrils? The spirit of life. The word *ruach* in Hebrew is the same word used for the Spirit of God in Genesis 1:2. Man, unlike the animals, has the spirit of life in him. Man has a physical form, a soul, and spirit. He is both a physical being as well as a spiritual being. Because he is both a spiritual and physical being, he is not an evolved animal. The man God created was unlike the physical animals and angels who are spiritual. It is essential to know that man and animal are not even close to being the same. Take some time to read 1 Thessalonians 5:23. What does it say about you?

Week 26, Day 3

The Lord God planted a garden…

Do you remember the day you first bought your pet? Get a piece of paper and list everything you had to buy to have a pet. That's a lot of stuff. Why did you need all those items? Because you had to create the perfect environment for them to live in. Even though they live in a great place like your home, they wouldn't survive if they didn't have a place made just for them despite being loved and cared for. God had created a perfect world. But when He brought forth His highest and most unique creation, humanity, He did something different. God prepared a special place for man to live, different from the rest of creation. He planted a garden. Jump ahead in the Bible and read John 14:1-3. As you read this, your Lord Jesus is preparing a perfect place for you to live in His Father's house. One day He will return for you so you can always be with Him. The story of God's relationship with man begins and ends with man living in a place perfectly prepared by God. Aren't you grateful that God loves you so much that He is preparing a perfect place for you?

Week 26, Day 4

The Lord God planted a garden…

Not all gardens are the same. There are herb, vegetable, flower, and tropical gardens. But one garden that catches everyone's eye is an ornamental garden. An ornamental garden design includes flowering plants and bulbs and foliage plants, grasses, shrubs, and trees—beautiful flowers, budding trees, and wispy grasses all blend for an eye-pleasing picture. The key is planning and planting. You place each plant in such a manner that every visitor sees it in its best setting. It is incredible how much effort gardeners put into planting a garden. How much more do you think the Creator of the universe put into planting a garden? It would be hard to imagine the garden's beauty and provision. Each item was planted by the same "hands" that had formed the man. How would it appear if you were going to design the perfect place for you to live?

Week 26, Day 5

The Lord God planted a garden...

There was once a little boy who lived in paradise. One of his favorite places to play was an area called Bluerock. There was a creek that flowed through the valley that had blue shale rock formations. You could find fossils, play in the creek, catch crawdads, and the shale rocks skipped the water perfectly. Forty years before that time, there was a golf course on that land. But there was no evidence that a golf course ever existed. After many years of living in other places, the boy returned to Bluerock. As he walked to where he knew it would be, he found not a creek but a vast lake. A dam had been built, and a lake covered the entire area where he used to play. There was no evidence that Bluerock ever existed. Paradise was lost forever. Today you begin our study of the Garden of Eden. It was a paradise that existed just for God's highest creation, man. There is no physical evidence that it ever existed. No point on the map where you can go and say there it was. Paradise was lost forever, and the story of Eden is how it happened.

Week 26, Day 6

…and there He placed the man…

Back in your study, you uncovered the Principles for Living Holy. These principles were the personal attributes of God. You also saw those same attributes in the man God created in His image. In Genesis 1:14-15, you discovered the principle of Purpose. God only acts with purpose. Whatever He does is intentional, not random. So in verse 2:8, when it says He placed the man in Eden, it was not like putting something on a shelf and walking away only to forget where you put it. God had a purpose for placing man in the garden. It is interesting to note that the Hebrew word for paradise is Eden. Why would God put man, made in His image, in a place entirely created for him? What purpose would God have to position man with the same attributes as Himself in such an ideal setting? Why do you think God did this?

Week 27, Day 1

...and there He placed the man...

Today explore some passages of Scripture. They all have a purpose – to reveal the purpose for which God placed the man created in His image in a perfect paradise. There are several passages. Carefully read them all before going on. Genesis 6:9-21, Genesis 22:2-14, Exodus 16:11-27, and Deuteronomy 2:7. Put on your detective hat and examine what you have read. What are some things that are common to all these passages? Who are the people involved in the stories? What was their relationship with the Lord? What were they asked to do? When did the action occur? How were they affected by what happened? Why do you think they were in these situations?

Week 27, Day 2

…and there He placed the man…

You have probably already figured out the answer to the question of why God placed man in the Garden of Eden. But read one more verse for each of the stories you read yesterday. Genesis 6:22, Genesis 22:1, Exodus 16:4, and Deuteronomy 8:2. God placed man, created in His image, in the garden's ideal setting, for one purpose – to test him. God never leaves faithfulness and obedience unmeasured. There is always a test. God made sure everything was perfect for man. God made provision for everything. He even gave man His own attributes. The greatest of which was the free will to decide. Now He will test the faithfulness of all mankind.

Week 27, Day 3

…and there He placed the man…

What you learned yesterday could be a little hard to believe. Some might say this is Old Testament theology, and God deals differently with people because of Jesus. Take time to read three stories from the New Testament. Matthew 4:1-11, Mark 1:12-13, and Luke 4:1-13. What do the stories share about Jesus? How does Jesus end up in the wilderness? Who else is in the story? What happens to Jesus while He is in the desert? If God tested Adam, Noah, Abraham, the Israelites, and even His only begotten Son, what do you think is in store for you? Read these two passages, 1 Peter 4:12-13 and James 1:2-4. What do you learn about the importance of God's testing?

Week 27, Day 4

...and there He placed the man...

No matter what language you study, there is a way of making the reader or hearer distinguish between a general group of items and a specific item. It is called a definite article. In English, it is the difference between "a" and "the." Look in Genesis 2:8. Notice the phrase, "He placed the man whom He had formed." It is crucial to remember these are the very words of God, exact in every way. He does not say "a" man, anyone selected of many, but "the" man. The only one He formed. God clearly states that He created and placed one man in the Garden of Eden. People often say phrases such as, "Which came first, the chicken or the egg?" You know that God created the animals first. The animal then produced the egg. But their underlying question says, "You don't know how it all began." But you do. All the people you now see on this planet came from one man, formed by God from the earth and placed in a perfect place. You now refer to him as Adam, based on the Hebrew word for man.

Week 27, Day 5

Out of the ground the Lord God caused to grow…

There are several methods God used in His creation. First, He spoke things into existence from nothing. Then, He formed items from already created matter. Finally, He planted a particular garden in which to place Adam. And now, in verse nine, He "causes to grow" every tree. At first, you may think that God miraculously, outside the expected growth, caused the tree to appear. And that could certainly be true. Yet everything God has created was designed with its processes already in existence. Vegetation, birds, sea creatures, and animals all have an internal process that allows them to grow. They survive and thrive on their own without someone causing them to grow. But what is this passage saying? God planted the garden so that He caused specific trees to grow in particular locations. If you decide to plant a pear tree three feet from the north corner of your driveway, you have caused it to grow where? God planned and planted His garden for a particular purpose.

Week 27, Day 6

…every tree that is pleasing to the sight and good for food…

The trees of the garden had two particular qualities. First, the trees were pleasant to the sight. Of who, God or Adam, maybe both? Trees in the garden are the first created item that had beauty. All things are good, but now a quality draws Adam's attention. The eyes of man, created by God, have a desire for beauty. Thomas Dubai says in the title of his book there is power in beauty. Nobel Prize-winning physicist Richard Feynman said, "You can recognize truth by its beauty and its simplicity." God so created man that he would be drawn to beauty. The word translated as "pleasing" is defined as to delight in. Think about a sunset, a flower, the freshly mowed yard, the sight of an old friend, a child willingly doing what is asked, a table filled with food, and family seated all around. The desire for what is pleasing in your sight reminds you that God delights in the same things. Read Hebrews 13:21 and 1 John 3:22.

Week 28, Day 1

...the tree of life...and the tree of knowledge of good and evil.

The definition of a literary device is a technique a writer uses to produce a particular effect in their writing. An example of a literary device is a flashback, where the reader is carried back in time. What you have today in 3:9 is a literary device called foreshadowing. It is when the author shares something unexplained at the time that will become very important in the future. The Bible tells us that the garden also contained two exceptional trees. The first was called the tree of life. The second is the tree of knowledge of good and evil. At the point they are introduced, nothing is said of their significance. But later on, you will find out that they will play a massive role in the most significant event in the history of humanity. In the Bible, because it is the very words of God, there are no insignificant parts. All Scripture is God-breathed and is, therefore, significant.

Week 28, Day 2

...God planted a garden toward the east, in Eden...

Read Genesis 2:8,10-14. In the 1950s, education and faith had a secure connection. When classmates arrived at school every morning, they stood and said the Pledge of Allegiance and then recited the Lord's Prayer. Not everyone was a Christian, but everyone acknowledged God's role in their lives. The system of education had a Biblical worldview. The Bible was seen as being accurate and had a significant influence on teaching. It now seems hard to believe. In history lessons of that day, the beginning of humanity was in a specific location. That location was the Fertile Crescent between the Tigris and the Euphrates Rivers. It was called the Cradle of Civilization. Why do you think this was taught? In your verses for today, there are current names of rivers. So naturally, education associated Eden with recent locations on the map. But is that the truth? What was the exact description of the Garden of Eden site in the verses you read?

Week 28, Day 3

…God planted a garden toward the east, in Eden…

Today take time to draw a map. Cartography is the science or practice of drawing maps. Today you have Google Earth to show you locations anywhere in the world. You have Google Maps to get directions showing you how to get to any place you want. But those maps can't tell you where something existed long ago. Cities have come and gone over the centuries. Their locations have shifted due to natural disasters, wars, and economics. When you study the past, you need to use the records of that time to reconstruct their location maps. Get out a piece of paper and draw a map based on the information in Genesis 2:8,10-14.

Week 28, Day 4

...God planted a garden toward the east, in Eden...

How does your map look? Search the internet for a "Map of the Garden of Eden." How did they compare to your map? Did you agree with any of their interpretations of Genesis? What did you find familiar in their charts? They all want to place the Garden on a current world map. They want to associate the rivers and countries with the existing names of locations. Did you do that with your drawing? Why? Possibly you think of the earth as always looking as it does now. But remember the account of creation. Genesis 1:9 says that all the waters are gathered together in one location, and the dry land appears. Are all the waters of the earth in one place today? The world was perfect, watered from the earth, not the sky. The world looked very different in the days of creation.

Week 28, Day 5

...God planted a garden toward the east, in Eden...

Just like with any instructions, context plays a big part. When re-creating the oldest map in history, there are some things to consider. The first choice you need to make is to orient your paper to the north. Now where to begin? The Bible says the garden was "in Eden to the east." The location is in a particular section of Eden. Therefore the boundaries of Eden must be larger than the Garden. Now place the Garden on the east side of Eden. Next, the Bible says a river flows out of Eden to water the garden. How do you show a river flowing out of Eden into the Garden? In the garden, one river divides into four rivers. The question has to be which way and how far they went. How does it look in comparison to the original drawing you made?

Week 28, Day 6

...God planted a garden toward the east, in Eden...

You have done something exceptional. You have just recreated the oldest map ever recorded. Your map is the account by God of the first map He ever gave man. But as you have already discovered, the geography of the land it was written for no longer exists. There are names similar to the names you use today, such as Tigris and Euphrates, along with an area called Assyria. But that does not mean they exist in the exact location that they do now. If you were to say you were born in Charleston, it wouldn't be all that specific. There are 22 cities in the United States named Charleston and many more in other countries. Though our described map is accurate according to the time it represented, the locations cannot be found today. Paradise, Eden, in Hebrew, has been lost. But Jesus says to the thief beside Him on the cross, "Today, you will be with Me in Paradise." Where do you think that may be?

Week 29, Day 1

Then the Lord God...

Look at the importance of language in Genesis 2:15. Then the LORD God _____ the man and ____ him into the garden of Eden to _____ it and _____ it. You will notice that some words have been left out of the text. First, think about what the words might be. Based on what you have learned from our previous study, what do you think the words might be? What does it imply that God did with the man? What do you think the man was supposed to do in the garden? The original words are in Hebrew, not English. Translation creates one of the most significant difficulties for Bible scholars. For the next few days, you will investigate how important proper translation is to Bible study. What words would you put in the blanks without looking in the Bible?

Week 29, Day 2

Then the Lord God…

One of the incredible things about Bible study today is the number of translations. Find as many interpretations of Genesis 2:15. You may have several in your home. Collect all the different translations you can find. One of the great ways is to access Bible Gateway online. They have many Bible translations. Write in the blank spaces of Genesis 2:15 the words you find in the translations. How many of them match? Did any of them match your words? A group of highly educated men and women have devoted much of their lives to present you with an accurate translation. That group carefully selected every word. When you see different phrases, it doesn't mean one is wrong and the other right. It means that they interpret the meaning of the same Hebrew word differently. Now select the word you think best to fill in the blanks.

Week 29, Day 3

Then the Lord God...

The first step in Bible translation is to know the words you are attempting to translate. If you only have the word in English, it is like having the answer, but you don't know the question. The language in which the Old Testament is written is Hebrew. Unlike English, Hebrew is written from right to left. Also, you read it from what you would call the back of the book to the front. The letters are quite different but are placed in words just as they are in English. So how can you find out what word, translated into English in your Bible, was the word originally written in Hebrew? Especially since you cannot read Hebrew. You can thank James Strong, who published <u>Strong's Concordance</u> in 1890. His work was a fantastic accomplishment. He took every Hebrew and Greek word used initially in the Bible and gave it a number. Then he linked that number to the corresponding English word in the King James Bible. So by looking at his concordance, you can discover the original word. Today almost all Bible study aids you use are linked to Mr. Strong's Concordance.

Week 29, Day 4

Then the Lord God...

Now let's look at the actual words: *Laqach* translated as took, *nuach* as placed, *abad* as cultivate and *shamar* as keep. Did your study reveal other ways that these words might be translated? It can be pretty interesting how many ways a word can be interpreted. As you have studied before, context is one of the most important things to consider. For example, if a friend tells you "I love you" and then says the exact words to their spouse, do they mean the same thing? No, as much as a friend loves you, it is far different when the other person is a spouse. The Bible says a husband and wife are one. The word *nuach* is interesting because it means "to rest, to remain, to be quiet." How do 'to rest' and 'to put' go together? In what way might you translate this word for better understanding?

Week 29, Day 5

The Lord God took the man and put him in the garden of Eden.

Have you ever heard someone say, "That's bad," when they mean it was good? It is not the word that conveys the thought; it is the context. Bad can mean good in a specific context. The word *nuach* in Genesis 2:15 is in the context of being placed in a particular place, the garden. It is where the man was to live ultimately, where he was to remain. But the man didn't choose that place; God did. God put him in the home that He had created just for the man. The man was resting in the place God had prepared. Read Hebrews 4:9-10. Therefore there remains a Sabbath rest for the people of God. The one who has entered His rest has rested himself from his works, as God did from His. Just as God rested (Sabbath) from what He had done, man rests (nuach) in what He has done.

Week 29, Day 6

...to cultivate it...

You call places where people service cars service stations. When you go to dinner, the person who brings you food is a server. When the ball is put into play in a tennis match, it is served. These are all ways of using the word serve or, as you learned from our study of the word *abad*. In each case, the one who provides service works. That work usually has a name to describe the type of work done. A person who works on a car is a mechanic, a restaurant worker is a waiter, and someone in a tennis match is a player. If you were to describe their work, you would say they repair the car, wait on customers, and play tennis. What word would describe serving or working in a garden? You could say cultivate, plant (except you know God planted), plow, till, dig, nurture, or tend. Did the garden serve the man, or did the man serve the garden? What word would you use here?

Week 30, Day 1

...and keep it.

The last word is *shamar*. The word is used 468 times in the Bible. Because the Bible uses it in so many contexts, it translates in many ways. The King James Bible uses 72 different words to translate *shamar*. Pretty impressive. In translating the Bible, the translators are trying to get one word in English for one Hebrew word. But many times, it is not possible. Other translations, such as the Amplified Bible, try to give more sense or understanding of the translation. The word *shamar* translates most often as to guard or to keep. If you only wanted to interpret the word, either of those two words would suffice. But what did God mean by having the man guard or keep the garden? Imagine you were asked to hold someone's car until they returned. What would that mean? You wouldn't want it stolen while you guarded it, but you do not wish to stand and look at it all the time. You wouldn't want it wrecked but would like to use it. If you did use it, you would put gas and oil in it. You would treat it like you owned it. In short, you were being asked to be responsible for the car. So what do you think God wanted Adam to be for the garden?

Week 30, Day 2

…and keep it.

Halacha is the name for Jewish religious law. It is often translated as "the path or way one should walk." It is a compilation of oral and written traditions based on the Torah. As you learned earlier, all Hebrew words are derived from a three-letter word, the base verb form. The word you learned yesterday is *shamar* is the base form verb to guard or keep. God has charged Adam to *shamar* the garden. What is most interesting is that a *shomer* is the noun form of that verb. In the *Halacha*, a *shomer* is a legal guardian entrusted with another's object's custody and care. Adam is now the legal guardian of God's garden. He does not own the garden, but he is responsible for the garden.

Week 30, Day 3

...and keep it.

Matthew 22:29 But Jesus answered and said to them, "You are mistaken, not understanding the Scriptures nor the power of God." Jesus spoke to men who had devoted their lives to studying the Scriptures. Can you imagine how disappointing it would be for them to hear this? Also, what about all the people they had taught? They were taught incorrectly and possibly believed things that were not entirely true. The responsibility is solemn for those who teach God's word. James 3:1 says, "Let not many of you become teachers, my brethren, knowing that as such you will incur a stricter judgment." Today you may have learned something by reading the Bible that has changed your understanding of the Scriptures. It will affect how you teach from this point forward. The encouragement is that you will always find new understanding no matter how long you read His word. Don't ever think you have learned it all. Keep studying, ask questions, and be careful when teaching what you believe the Bible says. Endeavor always to ensure you KNOW what the Biblical text means.

Week 30, Day 4

The Lord God commanded…

Do you remember the first words God ever said to humankind? That's right, "Be fruitful and multiply, and fill the earth, and subdue it." God also gave humanity provisions to survive. God said in Genesis 1:29, "Behold, I have given you every plant yielding seed that is on the surface of all the earth, and every tree which has fruit yielding seed; it shall be food for you." How important is food to you? You must have food to live. But in addition to that, it is delicious. People love to eat. The food shows on TV are top-rated. There are entire channels devoted to nothing but a tremendous variety of food. Here is a question for you, "Do you eat to live, or do you live to eat?" Did God make food attractive so you would eat it, or are you attracted to it because it is necessary to survive? It probably depends on how hungry you are and how well the food is prepared. The point of eating is not only essential but also desirable. When it is good, you certainly want it.

Week 30, Day 5

The Lord God commanded…

What if there were no consequences for any decisions you made? Wouldn't it be great if the result was perfect every time you had to choose? Everything went perfectly. Everybody was happy with your choice, and the results matched what you wanted to happen. Wonder why, if God loved you, He did not make it that way? Why are there good and bad decisions? As you have learned, man is in God's image and free to choose. God did not create robots to do his bidding. Man was created for fellowship with God. God desired this relationship to be voluntary on the man's part. Not because the man had to love God but because he wanted the relationship. But the issue is that it can only happen if people are free to choose. Only if there are consequences can right and wrong be determined. You can only choose correctly if you are free to choose incorrectly.

Week 30, Day 6

The Lord God commanded…

Have you ever had someone try to get you to do something you know is wrong? Someone you considered a friend asked you to do something you knew was wrong. You are confronted with having to make a choice. Either you do what your friend asks or refuse to go along. The results of your decision will bring about some consequences. If you say yes, you will have disobeyed your conscience. If you say no, your friend will be angry at you, and you may lose a friend. How do you make such an important decision? Most often, you make decisions based on the outcome. You consider questions like these. What do I want most? What do I think is best? How will this turn out? What's the downside? These are all very reasonable questions for those who don't have a relationship with Jesus. But these are not the right question for believers. The best question you can ask yourself is, "How do I love?" Obedience. Jesus says in John 14:15, "If you love Me, you will keep My commandments." The Bible clearly states that you are to obey God's word. But how do you love your friends? Truth. Ephesians 4:15 says, "Speaking the truth in love." You must tell your friend, "The truth is that what you ask me to do is not God's best for either of us." Never be afraid of telling the truth. The most important question to ask yourself in every moral decision is, "In this situation, how do I love?"

Week 31, Day 1

…"From any tree of the garden you may eat freely, but…

In Genesis 2:16-17, there is an instruction, which the Bible calls a command, with a different twist. First, it reiterates a previous confirmation of what the man can eat. But then God mentions one tree that is not available for food, the tree of knowledge of good and evil. How man identifies that tree or where it is in the garden God does not share. Suffice it to say there was a way to know the tree because eating it would result in death. There is a fruit called Manchineel fruit that grows in the Caribbean and Florida. It is called "the little apple of death." Wikipedia reveals when ingested, the fruit is "pleasantly sweet" at first, with a subsequent "strange peppery feeling…, gradually progress[ing] to a burning, tearing sensation and tightness of the throat". Symptoms continue to worsen until the patient can "barely swallow solid food because of the excruciating pain and the feeling of a huge obstructing pharyngeal lump." The Manchineel is not the tree of the knowledge of good and evil, but it is a real tree. It teaches us that even though things look good, they are not always good for us. Would you eat this fruit? Who would ever taste the fruit that you know would kill you?

Week 31, Day 2

…you shall not eat…

How important is it to memorize Scripture, word for word? Wouldn't it be OK if you get close? Isn't it just the idea you are trying to capture, not every little word? So what if you add a word here or there or leave a word out? It is the intention of your heart, not the exact wording. Look at a simple verse. 1 Timothy 6:10 says, "For the love of money is a root of all sorts of evil, and some by longing for it have wandered away from the faith and pierced themselves with many griefs." You have heard other people quote this verse. I bet you heard them say, "Money is the root of all evil." Which it does say if you leave out "the love of." Money is neutral; it is a thing to be used. It becomes a problem when you love it. You might also say the love of money produces greed. But that is not the warning the text gives. The warning is that you are in danger of wandering away from the faith and piercing yourself with grief. You see how important it is to know the exact word as it is. These are the very words of God, the Creator. In the story of Adam, you will see the extreme importance of knowing exactly what God said.

Week 31, Day 3

...you will surely die.

Have you ever had someone in authority tell you to do something that, at the time, made no sense? There was no explanation, just a command to do something. For example, on a bright sunny day, you are driving down a road, and suddenly there is a policeman who says, "Stop, turn around, and go the other way. You would be in danger of great harm if you continued." You would, of course, wonder why? What kind of danger? Was it that bad? But because of the authority of the one giving you the command, you obeyed immediately. There was no explanation of why the man would die if he ate of the tree. Only the character, knowledge, and authority of the one sharing the information existed. That is why it is so vital that you obey God. You know his character, you are assured of His knowledge of the situation, and you are always subject to His authority. When His word tells you that His best for you is to behave in a certain way, you should follow His instruction immediately, just as He says, and with a right heart attitude. You will see the results of the man's decision in days to come.

Week 31, Day 4

…you will surely die.

At this point, on the sixth day of creation, the man is alone in the garden. At this point, he has not spoken. All communication has come from God, his Creator. Let's review what the man knows from God. Only what Genesis 2:15-17 relates. The information in chapter one, multiplication, ruling, and subduing, is only given after the female is on the scene. Therefore, the man is the only person who heard God's commandment concerning eating the tree of knowledge of good and evil. What is your responsibility if you are the only one who knows something is harmful? Right, to tell others. The man was solely responsible for "teaching her to observe all that I commanded." Sound familiar? Right, it is from the great commission in Matthew 28. This concept is the foundation of God's way of transferring faith through discipleship. Those who know teach those who do not know. Parents disciple their children, one generation guides the next generation, wise leaders instruct the people, prophets warn the nations, Jesus teaches twelve, and the followers of Christ make disciples. So what is your responsibility?

Week 31, Day 5

...It is not good...

Genesis 2:18 God said, "It is not good." For the first time in the creation story, you hear something "not good." Until this point, everything is considered acceptable. Did God create something that is not good? Did God make a mistake in the creation of man? Did God have to see how things were going for the man before he realized something wasn't right? God knew His creation and provided what the man needed from the garden's trees. Now God demonstrates that He knows what His creation requires. He, therefore, provides the greatest gift to man, intimate companionship. This relationship was necessary to complete humanity. Without this companionship, the man would be incomplete. When God said it was not right, He wasn't saying something wrong or bad had come into creation. He was saying that the creation was not complete. For the man to be complete as God desired, there had to be someone "suitable for him."

Week 31, Day 6

…It is not good…

Look into a mirror. What do you see? You see yourself, duh! But what is different? First, everything is on the other side. In the mirror, the right is left, and the left is right. Also, the front is back, and the back is front. The figure is facing the opposite way. You, of course, cleverly call this a mirror image. Now imagine that what you are looking at is another person. A real live person, but in every way opposite of you. Everything you see one way, they perceive the opposite. Everything you think, they think the other. You see a beautiful sunset; they see good weather tomorrow. You see rain; they see flowers growing. You see old; they see wisdom. Now because of culture, you immediately think of competition. This person is always opposite to me, and they are against me. But what if they weren't? What if they were there to help you in every way? What you miss, they see. What you can't understand, they do. What you can't, they can. In every way you are deficient, they are sufficient. Where they lack, you have an abundance. They would, in essence, complete you. You would not be two halves, but together you would be whole. Genesis 2:18 says, Then the LORD God said, "It is not good for the man to be alone; I will make him a helper suitable for him."

Week 32, Day 1

Out of the ground, the Lord God formed...

How do you think God will make a helper suitable for the man? Read Genesis 2:19. Wait a minute, didn't God already create all the beasts of the field and birds of the sky? Before the creation of humanity, God formed all the beasts of the fields. God had formed the birds on the fifth day. But this is not a passage indicating order but confirmation. The verse better reads, "Out of the ground the Lord God had already formed..." God brings all the created kinds to the man. Why? If the man was to first rule over all the creation, naming the animals was up to him. In Hebrew thought, authority is shown by naming something or someone. Secondly, it is man's responsibility to find a suitable helper. In this menagerie of creatures, the man was to choose one. God presents the man with his first test, finding a helper suitable for him from all the creation.

Week 32, Day 2

…out of the ground the Lord God formed…

Until now, the man has not seen that God has created anything. Everything was already created when the man came on the scene. The creation is complete. He could look around and see what God had already done but had not seen God create. The man must ask himself, how did all this get here? What is it for? But rather than explaining, God begins to share everything He has made. He brings all the created animals before his ultimate creation, man. Have you ever had someone show their new home to you? Or has anyone ever shared their collection of items? What are they doing? They are honoring you with what they deem valuable. They consider you worthy of sharing their possessions. God has regarded as worthy the man to share His possessions. Now man stands as the pinnacle of all that God has created.

Week 32, Day 3

…to see what he would call them…

One of the great joys of life is having a pet. What's the first thing you do when you get a pet dog, cat, fish, or bird? Right, you name it. It is your choice. Sometimes you make up a name, call it by some pet characteristic, or even give it someone in the family's name. What's the next thing you do? You provide for it. You begin the process of gathering all the things your pet needs. You will need food, water, a place to sleep, and something with which to play. There is a lot to gather. Why? Because with authority comes responsibility. When you are given authority over something, you become responsible for it. Since you have authority, whatever happens to your pet becomes your responsibility. You are accountable for its well-being. If you fail to fulfill our obligation, your pet suffers. Imagine the great responsibility of the man. There was probably great joy in naming the animals, hoping to find a helper suitable for him. But at some point, he had to think, "How am I going to take care of all this?" Remember, authority always requires responsibility.

Week 32, Day 4

…to see what he would call them…

An intriguing phrase occurs in Genesis 2:19. It says that God brought the living creatures to the man "to see" what he would call them, which would become their name. That phrase for us would mean observing an outcome of which you are uncertain. When you go to a ballgame, or movie, or even look outside at the weather, you are looking to see what will happen with no ability to influence the outcome. Is that what God is doing? Does He not know how the naming of the animals will occur? Did the man name one creature a hippopotamus, and God said, "I never thought of that!" Was God surprised by the names that the man chose? Not at all. God is omnipotent. He knows all things. Remember what is genuinely occurring here. The man was to search for a "helper suitable." Good fathers place their children in situations where the father knows the outcome to see how their children handle the situation. God knows that the man will not find a suitable helper. But the man doesn't know. God could have just told him that, but it is always better for your children to find out for themselves. The exercise of naming animals was not about naming animals but about the man discovering nothing in all the creation that would complete him. Do you think God watches you today "to see" how you search the creation for something to complete you?

Week 32, Day 5

…to see what he would call them…

Every parent wants to have intelligent children. One of the ways is to teach them to speak at an early age. Usually, you show them cards with pictures of animals. You generally make the animal's sound, and the child imitates you. Then, gradually, you introduce the animal's name, and they, too, begin to say it. How did God bring everything into existence? By the words of His mouth. When He spoke into existence the species giraffe, what do you think He said?" Let there be an armadillo?" No, He said, "Let there be a giraffe." When He told the man to name the species, what do you think the man said the species' name was? As a parent with a child, God showed the man the item to see if he knew the name God had given it in creation. By naming the animals, the man took authority over them, but only because He agreed with God on the name already given. Remember, this was not an exercise in naming but in finding a helper suitable for the man.

Week 32, Day 6

…to see what he would call them…

In the Hebrew language, the word for man, mankind, and Adam are all the same, Adam. But here, the man is referred to as Adam for the first time in the Bible. Just like with God earlier using His name LORD, Adam is known by his name. But at this point, he is still alone with God. The search for a helper suitable for him has ended. No living creature was found to be a match for Adam. One day that journey in search of the perfect match begins for every person. The desire for a lifelong companion will become an all-consuming task, just like Adam naming the animals. How will you make that decision? What criteria will you use? How will you know when you find the one suitable for you? Fortunately, just like in Adam's case, you are not the only one working on this situation. God, the great provider, is preparing a suitable helper. Adam only had to know that he could not find one independently. The truth is neither can you.

Week 33, Day 1

So the Lord God caused a deep sleep...

Ether is a gas that "puts people to sleep" during a medical procedure. When they are under the influence of ether, they do not feel pain or remember what has happened. A dentist named William T. G. Morton was the first person to use ether in 1846. It revolutionized medical procedures by eliminating pain for a patient. The patient loses awareness, yet his vital functions, such as breathing and blood pressure maintenance, continue to function. The fantastic thing is that God demonstrated this long before Dr. Morton. Genesis 2:21 says, "So the LORD God caused a deep sleep to fall upon the man, and he slept." There are two words used for sleep in this sentence. The first means causing someone to become deeply unaware. The second word means to sleep naturally. Despite the honor Dr. Morton received being the first to use anesthesia, God preceded him by many centuries. Sometimes you can think you are the first ever to create something. But you must be reminded of what Solomon says, "There is nothing new under the sun."

Week 33, Day 2

He took one of his ribs...

Take time for a little review. How were all the living creatures created? They were spoken into existence by God. But notice from where they came. In every case, living creatures, including man, are from the earth or ground. In Genesis 2:21, God is taking the matter for creating, not from the creation, but from the created. It says God took from Adam "one of the ribs." The word used here can be translated as rib or side. But that's not what is essential. It was necessary to create a helper suitable for Adam. The "rib" could not be taken from the earth. God had to take it from the man. Whatever God was making for man, it was from a man. All humanity would descend from Adam. The nature of Adam would be in all humanity, save One.

Week 33, Day 3

The Lord God fashioned...

Genesis 2:22 is another first for the Bible; the LORD God fashioned. You might think fashioned is the same word as made or formed. But it is not at all; it means to build. It is used quite often in the Bible to describe the construction of buildings. But here is its only use concerning life. Remember, as you have seen, the Bible is particular in what it says, even scientifically. God chooses to use a word uniquely. From what is life created? Cells: The Building Blocks of Life! The Cell Theory states that all living things are built of cells, the basic units of life and that cells come from other cells. How are those cells produced? Deoxyribonucleic Acid (DNA) is comprised of chemical building blocks called nucleotides. These building blocks are composed of three parts: a phosphate group, a sugar group, and one of four nitrogen bases. DNA was first identified in the late 1860s by Swiss chemist Friedrich Miescher. Could it be that the LORD God knew that man would one day discover His creation of DNA? Then when men in the future read about creating a helper suitable. He would understand being "built" from man's DNA rather than made or formed.

Week 33, Day 4

The Lord God fashioned…

God fashioned "a woman." The word is the first time this title appears for a living creature. In Chapter 1, God used the title female. Then, after building a woman, God brought her to the man. Remember the purpose? To find a helper suitable for Adam. Now just as God had also brought all the living creatures for man first, to find a helper suitable, then to see what he would name her. Would she be suitable, and would he choose the same name that God had already given? Remember, Adam has been unaware during this process.

Week 33, Day 5

The man said…

Your assignment today is to find out about the day you were born. It may require calling your parents. Ask these questions. What did you say the first time you saw me? What thoughts went through your mind as you held me for the first time? What was the most fantastic thing about my birth? The birth of a child is the closest you can come to what it was like the first time Adam saw the Woman. It will help if you read his words with great excitement. The same way people respond to the birth of their child. Read what Adam said with that feeling. Adam expresses his amazement: "Finally, after all this searching for a helper suitable for me, I found the perfect one because she is bone of my bone, flesh of my flesh." 1 Corinthians 15:39 says, "All flesh is not the same flesh, but there is one flesh of men, and another flesh of beasts, and another flesh of birds, and another of fish." The Woman was of the same flesh as Adam.

Week 33, Day 6

She shall be called woman…

Why is always the best question. It forces us to give a reason for our behavior. Most of the time, people don't express their reasons for doing something. They just do it. But in the story, Adam explains why he named God's helper suitable for him, woman. It was because she was taken out of him. The name for a male or a husband in Hebrew is *ish*. The name for a female or wife is *ishshah*. Adam's name for the suitable helper comes from the word, which describes himself. This unique creation of the woman, as listed in Genesis 1:27, means that humanity is only complete if males and females exist.

Week 34, Day 1

For this reason…

The next verse, Genesis 2:24, reveals that all God has done makes sense. It begins with the summary phrase, "For this reason." When studying the Bible, always be aware of summary phrases. They give you the reason things happen—phrases like so that, in order to, for this reason, therefore. When you see these words, you know what comes next summarizes the previously discussed. It also shares the reason for the events. Read verse 24 by replacing the phrase "For this reason" with "Because mankind is only complete when there is both male and female…" Generally, these summary phrases are the most crucial part of your study.

Week 34, Day 2

...a man shall leave his father and mother, and be joined to his wife...

What is God's best for humanity? As you have seen throughout the creation story, God has created humankind for a relationship with Him. But what is God's best for man's relationship with each other? What is your favorite food? What movie do you like most? What do you think is the most fantastic sport? What is most valuable in life? Where is your favorite place to go? These questions don't mean all other things are worthless. It just means, what do you think is best? In the origin story, God will share the best relationship for humanity. It does not mean it is the only relationship in life. There are beautiful friendships with others. It merely means the marriage of a man and woman is the best relationship for humanity in God's plan.

Week 34, Day 3

…and they shall become one…

God's best for humanity begins with understanding who God is. Moses gave them fundamental instructions when God's chosen people were about to enter the promised land. They are in Deuteronomy 6:4-9. Today read that passage. Now list what you learn about God Himself in this passage. There is only one character trait listed in the passage. "The Lord is our God, the Lord is _____." The Hebrew word here is *echad*. It means oneness or unity. Strange description until you couple it with what you learned in Chapter 1 of Genesis. The Trinity, God, is Three in One. Remember the illustration of the lighted candle. Three distinct entities, all one at the same time. If God is One and humankind is in the image of God, what would be God's best for humanity?

Week 34, Day 4

...and they shall become one...

In a relationship like God, the *echad* (oneness) of male and female is the best for humanity. So how does that happen? This is very important. The foundation of what God desires for all humankind is in Genesis 2:24. But it begins with God's first command for humanity back in Genesis 1:22, "Be fruitful and multiply and fill the earth." At that point, God did not explain how that would happen. But now, one chapter later, He does. It begins in God's best relationship for humanity, a father and a mother. Most people would think it was a man and a woman. If humankind stayed husband and wife but never became father and mother, God's plan for humanity would never work. God's plan for humanity is entirely dependent physically and spiritually on fathers and mothers. The passage you read in Deuteronomy 6:4-9 is not written to individuals but to parents.

Week 34, Day 5

...and they shall become one...

God desired to fill the earth with humankind created in His image. How was that going to occur? Through parents, mothers, and fathers. But if you were to believe that parents' only purpose was to have children, you would be terribly mistaken. If that were true, the passage would say, "For this reason, a man shall be joined to his wife; and they shall be one flesh." Instead, it states, "a man shall leave his father and mother." God's design for the creation is the family. The institution of family was God's plan for all humanity, regardless of culture. God's best for humankind is the family unit, where sons and daughters live with their parents for a specified period. Why do you think that time was necessary?

Week 34, Day 6

...and they shall become one...

How did Adam know what his role was in the creation? Did it just come naturally? Maybe there was a knowledge placed in him that allowed him to understand what he was to accomplish. But if that were so, God would not need to explain Adam's purpose in creation. He would not have to be told to multiply, fill the earth, subdue, and rule over it. God wouldn't have to tell Adam what to eat, where to be, or how to relate to the creatures. God, the Father, had to instruct Adam in all the ways necessary for him to fulfill God's best for him and those who would be born to him. So, if God had to teach Adam how to achieve His best, what would Adam have to do for those born to him?

Week 35, Day 1

...and they shall become one...

As you learned from the very beginning, God created a self-perpetuating creation. He would never have to make another star, tree, creature, or man. God created a universe that would reproduce itself. The purpose of family, like the apple tree, was to produce more families. The only knowledge of how to best live would have to pass from generation to generation. The lion would not know how to hunt without its parents showing him how. So it would be for humanity. There would be a time when a boy would dwell with his parents. Then the day would come when he would leave his father and mother, cleave to his wife, and a new family would form. The most crucial time for any person would be the time under the nurture of their parents.

Week 35, Day 2

…and they shall become one…

Have you ever pulled a thread on your clothes? You find a string hanging, pull it, and suddenly you have a long thread unraveling from the cloth. You are going to pull a thread from the Bible today. That thread will run throughout the Bible. It starts with two words, father and mother. Three great Principles of Holy Living are contained in this thread that runs throughout the Bible. These three principles are the foundation for Godly family living. They are the principles of honor, submission, and procreation. Although the principles are throughout the Bible, you will use the Lord Jesus' teaching as your guide.

Week 35, Day 3

…and they shall become one…

Go on a scavenger hunt in search of a piece of plywood. It can be any old piece of any size. Lay the piece flat on a workbench or some support so that you can see the edge. You may have to take some sandpaper or file to clean off the edge to see it clearly. When you look at the side, what do you see? One piece or layers? Plywood is made by laying thin sheets of wood on each other with glue in between. Like a sandwich. Do you see the layers? The wood and glue are joined together under pressure. The result is that one piece of wood is much more durable than the thin layers. Now read Genesis 2:24. What does it say a man must do? Right be joined to his wife. The word translated "joined" is the Hebrew word for stick together. What does it say about the best relationship between a man and a woman?

Week 35, Day 4

…and they shall become one…

The word one, echad, is the same word that describes God. Like God, they, though being separate people, are joined and become united. God is defining marriage. Like the plywood is joined and becomes one, so do a man and a woman united in marriage become one. Take a putty knife and separate the layers of the plywood. Pull the sheets apart. What happens to the wood layers? They are splintered and destroyed. Once joined, they cannot separate without becoming less than they once were. This fragmenting is what divorce does to a marriage. Once a man and woman join together, they must never be separated. God's best for humanity is one man, and one woman joined together for a lifetime. One day you will make that decision. Remember the plywood.

Week 35, Day 5

...and they shall become one...

The first Family Principle of Holy Living comes in Matthew 15:4. What does Jesus say in this verse? Honor your father and mother. You will notice it is a quote from the Ten Commandments in chapter twenty of Exodus. Honoring your parents is the first step in fulfilling God's best desires for humanity. Children are to honor their parents. How is that accomplished? It means to value someone highly. In education, great teachers are highly valued. In sports, people highly value the actions of great athletes. In life, there is value in leadership. In the family, the foundation of all life, you must highly value your mother and father's teaching, actions, and leadership. Giving value to parents places them in the proper position in your life.

Week 35, Day 6

…and they shall become one…

The second family Principle of Holy Living comes in Luke 2:51. It is the principle of submission. This passage speaks of Jesus, the Son of God. What does it say about his relationship with his parents? It states that He continued in subjection to them. The word continued indicates He always considered Himself in subjection to His parents, Mary and Joseph. Jesus, the creator of all that is, subjected Himself to His parents. A person in the military is the best picture of what it means to be in submission. The most important thing for a soldier is to be in the right place at the right time, doing the right thing. How do they know what is right? They willingly place themselves under the authority of their commander to understand what is right. To fulfill what God says is best, children must voluntarily submit to the authority of their parents.

Week 36, Day 1

…and they shall become one…

The final family Principle of Holy Living is in the first phrase of Matthew 10:25. Jesus says, "It is enough for the disciple that he become like his teacher." To be a parent is more than just providing physical, mental, and emotional support for your children. Your most crucial role is the discipleship of your children. The model teacher of discipleship is Jesus. Parents' goal for their children must be to become like Him. Everything you share should be designed to encourage your children to be like Jesus. Discipleship is not what is taught; it is what is produced. Your greatest joy as a parent is when your children walk, speak, and interact with others, like Jesus. Every parent's desire must be for their children to be in the likeness and image of Jesus.

Week 36, Day 2

…and they shall become one flesh.

There is one area of Disneyworld that is as informative as it is enjoyable. It is Epcot Center. There you can see cultures from all over the world. It's incredible to see how different cultures use the same things differently. All the people speak, but they don't speak the same language. All people in the world eat but don't eat the same things. Everyone in the world dresses, but don't dress in the same clothes. But there is one thing that is the same in all cultures. Can you guess what it is? Right, it is family. The foundation of all cultures is family. There are differences in how families behave. But a family is always the same no matter where it is. It stems from Genesis 2:24. The family is the foundation of all society. No matter what government is in charge, what belief system is in place, and what is happening in that culture, the family is the same. Why? Because God created it that way. Most importantly, godly families are God's best for all humanity.

Week 36, Day 3

And the man and his wife…

Describe what the world would be like without sin. Get out a sheet of paper and write out a description of what it would be like to live in a world without sin. List the items you think would be different if there was no sin. For example, there would be no stealing if there were no sin. Therefore, you would not have to lock up everything. There would be no murder or assault; consequently, you wouldn't be afraid wherever you were. Make as long of a list as you like. Think of how often you have heard someone say, "All I want is world peace." Imagine a world where that was true. That was the world of the very first husband and wife.

Week 36, Day 4

And the man and his wife…

Revelation 21:3-4 describes this way. And I heard a loud voice from the throne, saying, "Behold, the tabernacle of God is among men, and He will dwell among them, and they shall be His people, and God Himself will be among them, and He will wipe away every tear from their eyes; and there will no longer be any death; there will no longer be any mourning, or crying, or pain; the first things have passed away." When God dwells in the world, the world is quite different. So now imagine the time of creation. Sin had not entered the world. None of the things you had to describe in yesterday's devotion had ever occurred. But there was one description that you probably left out. It sums up what the world was like with no sin. What might that be?

Week 36, Day 5

…both naked and were not ashamed.

Here is the phrase. Genesis 2:25 And the man and his wife were both naked and were not ashamed. A world without sin is innocence. Adam and Eve were entirely innocent. Their nakedness without shame is the perfect illustration of innocence. When you were little, you ran around naked. Your parents even took pictures of you. You did not feel ashamed or embarrassed. You were innocent. But now, if your parents shared that picture with your friends, what would you think? You see the difference sin brings. Sin shatters our innocence. Guilt and shame come when sin enters the world. The saddest time for you as a parent is to see your child's innocence lost. It was the same for your Heavenly Father.

Week 36, Day 6

...both naked and were not ashamed.

A second aspect of this passage stems from what you learned earlier. It concerns the physical appearance of the man and woman. In chapter one (Week 14, Day 2), you learned that God created them in His image. That image was one of light. All those who are in the presence of God are enclothed in light. Which means their appearance, unlike yours now, was one of light. Read what happened to Moses in Exodus 34:29-35, then Jesus at His transfiguration in Luke 9:28-32, and finally to those in heaven in Revelation 1:16. Light is not their clothing but their appearance. They are still naked. The Hebrew meaning is without covering. The bodies God has created have no covering. That will come later. For the present, they are like all those in God's presence, light.

Week 37, Day 1

…both naked and were not ashamed.

Reading takes you to places you have never been, visits worlds you will never see, introduces you to people you will never know and reveals truths you could never discover on your own. It pulls back the curtain on events that only those who participated in the story would know. You have now finished the story of how God created the heavens and the earth. Without this story, you would never know how life began. This grand narrative informs every person who reads it about the greatness of God and how He created humanity for fellowship with Him. Then how He gave humankind the authority over all His creation. And finally, how in absolute perfection and innocence all was finished. Even though it didn't rain, the earth was watered. The creation operated on its own with fabulous results. Humanity lived without guilt or shame. It was the perfect paradise. So why isn't it like that now?

Week 37, Day 2

…both naked and were not ashamed.

Have you ever put together a giant picture puzzle? How do you know where each piece fits? Usually, the first thing you look for is all the pieces with a straight edge, then you know it goes on the border. Next, you look for colors that match. Then you see if there are items in the picture that are similar. Finally, you try to get the different pieces to fit together. When the color, details, and shapes all match, you know you have the right piece. The outcome is a beautiful picture that matches the image you see on the outside of the box. But what if the picture doesn't match? You know that something went wrong. You may not know what happened, but you can quickly see they differ. That happens when you look at your world and the one God created. The picture in Genesis 1 and 2 does not match what you see in your world today. But what went wrong to make such a difference?

Week 37, Day 3

Now the serpent…

Today you enter the third chapter of Genesis. It begins with, "Now the serpent." Not a serpent, but The Serpent. This passage is not at all about snakes. This entity is a particular Serpent. Who is this Serpent? Until this point, how many individuals have you seen in the creation? God the Father, God the Son, God the Holy Spirit, Adam, and Eve. Read Ezekiel 28:11-19. Pay particular attention to the beginning of verse 13. What does it say? Wow, "You were in Eden, the garden of God." Ezekiel speaks to the King of Tyre in the sixth century BC, many years after the garden of Eden. In reality, Ezekiel isn't speaking of the king but someone whose character is like the king. God is using someone from the past as His example for the king to learn a lesson. It is like saying to someone losing faith in what they are doing, "you are like Peter walking on water." God is using the picture of one who was really in the garden. Who is this one?

Week 37, Day 4

Now the serpent...

Snakes are seldom anyone's favorite animal. The way they slither across the ground, hide under the brush, and present a constant danger in the woods is enough to cause people to shy away. But they are beautiful to observe. The way they glide without arms or legs, their colorful bodies, and their mesmerizing eyes make them quite stunning. But, of all the snakes you have ever seen, The Serpent is entirely different. Look at Ezekiel 28:12-13. Make a list of the items that describe the Serpent. Now try and draw a serpent that you see described. You might have to take time to discover the colors of the stones mentioned.

Week 37, Day 5

Now the serpent…

Ezekiel 28:14 tells you precisely who the Serpent is. Remember the discussion of the beings of the spiritual world that God created? Well, here is one—the anointed cherub who covers. Four cherubim surround the throne of God. The Serpent was one of them. How is he described? Full of wisdom and perfect in beauty. He was covered in precious stones and gold. What a sight he must have been. Until this point, the Bible says he was blameless from the moment he was created. This being, who dwelled in the very presence of God, has seen how God had carefully crafted the creation. He had seen the man and woman formed and the goodness of all that was made. But something was dreadfully wrong with him.

Week 37, Day 6

Now the serpent…

What does the Bible say about The Covering Cherub in Ezekiel 28:15? "Until unrighteousness was found in you." Something within the Cherub who lived in the very presence of God produced unrighteousness. "And you sinned." What is it that produced sin in the Cherub? Ezekiel 28:17 says, "Your heart was lifted up because of your beauty; You corrupted your wisdom by reason of your splendor." Ezekiel says that it was his heart that was lifted up. The Hebrew word indicates arrogant or proud. Pride was what produced the iniquity in The Serpent. Though he had all wisdom and beauty, formed in perfection, he became corrupt with sin. As you learned earlier, the spiritual beings God created could choose. The choice that The Serpent made was driven by pride. The question for you today is, "What drives your decisions?" Are your preferences founded in righteousness or unrighteousness?

Week 38, Day 1

Now the serpent...

Another passage that may give you insight into the actions of The Serpent comes in Isaiah 14:13-14. When Isaiah prophesied about the King of Babylon, he shared great discernment into the sin of pride. When pride entered The Serpent's heart, he desired to "make me like the Most High." When sin is in your heart, you want to be your own God, thereby rebelling against God, the Creator. One of the noteworthy parts of the passage is in verse 12. "Star of the Morning" is translated in Latin as Lucifer, another name for Satan. But the significance of this passage is the condition of rebellion against God's authority when sin enters a being, whether a cherub, an angel, or humanity. When sin is present, the desire is to be like the Most High. Thus a plan is hatched in the heart of The Serpent.

Week 38, Day 2

Now the serpent…

The last passage dealing with the identity of The Serpent is in the Revelation. Revelation 12:9 says, "And the great dragon was thrown down, the serpent of old who is called the Devil and Satan, who deceives the whole world; he was thrown down to the earth, and his angels were thrown down with him." John reveals the identity of The Serpent as the Devil, Satan—the covering cherub, dwelling in the very presence of God. Not only does the passage reveal his identity, but it also exposes a portion of his plan to make himself like the Most High. What does it say his intention is concerning the creation? Right, to deceive. Now you have a pretty complete picture of The Serpent. The question is, if God is all-powerful and all-knowing, how can Satan accomplish his plan?

Week 38, Day 3

Now the serpent…

There is a word that describes The Serpent's plan for creation, usurp, which means to take the place of someone in authority illegally. Take time to go back and read Genesis 1:26-28. What authority did God give to Adam? To rule over all the earth. God created and therefore owned all things, but He gave Adam the right to rule over all the earth. Satan knows he cannot overcome God. The Serpent only needs to usurp the authority of Adam to become the ruler of this world. How can he do this? What did you learn about The Serpent, Satan? He deceives the whole world. As you enter Chapter Three, you now know the evil one's plan. He will persuade Adam to give The Serpent the authority that rightfully belonged to Adam. Will it work? Will Adam give up rule over the earth to a deception?

Week 38, Day 4

Now the serpent…

Before you begin Chapter Three of Genesis, read this parable. Danny was going away for a year. He had a gorgeous boat. However, the craft must be taken out on the water each week for it to operate correctly. If not, the engine would cease to function correctly. Danny's best friend, George, lived next door to him on the lake. Danny gave George the keys to the boat with precise instructions on the required operation and maintenance. George was so happy that he could take such a beautiful boat out each week and ride around the lake. One day while riding out on the lake, he stopped by the marina. Sammy, the marina's owner, was outside and saw George in Danny's boat. He commented on how lucky he was to have the use of such a beautiful boat. George replied how much fun he was having, but his three-week vacation was coming soon. He shared what Danny had told him about the maintenance of the boat. Sammy told him, "That's what all the boat salespeople tell you, but that's just to sell you more stuff. It doesn't hurt a thing if you let the boat sit for a few weeks without running. Think of all the boats you see here in the marina that rarely go out on the lake." With that, George confidently left for vacation. Take time to identify Danny, George and Sammy based on the story of Genesis Three.

Week 38, Day 5

Now the serpent was more crafty...

Genesis 3:1. Now the serpent was more crafty than any beast of the field which the LORD God had made. The Hebrew word translated crafty is a fascinating word. It is a form of the English word "subtle." Subtle is defined as using clever and indirect methods to achieve something. The term is neutral in its meaning, neither good nor bad. On the one hand, it can mean to be prudent, but on the other, it could mean to be sly or crafty. The difference is the context. Since you know The Serpent's identity and his intention to deceive, it is translated as crafty, not prudent. The Serpent is full of wisdom. Wisdom is another neutral word. You generally think of wisdom as good, but you know Satan is about to use his wisdom for great evil. The same wisdom used to create nuclear energy could produce electricity or a bomb. The same wisdom used to finish an assigned task could be used to avoid being obedient. You are in the image of God, full of tremendous wisdom. How will you use that wisdom?

Week 38, Day 6

And he said to the Woman…

Read Genesis 2:15-28. What a statement! The Serpent spoke. It would help if you remembered that The Serpent is not a snake; he is the covering cherub. He is unique in all creation. But the fact that he speaks is not the most significant portion of this statement. The most crucial point is that he speaks to the Woman. When the deception begins, he addresses not Adam but the Woman. Remember, The Serpent is crafty, using an indirect method to achieve his end. He doesn't directly try to deceive Adam but indirectly attacks Adam through her. Remember that Adam is responsible for all creation, including his wife. Only Adam has heard the instructions of God concerning the tree of knowledge of good and evil. His responsibility was to share the truth of God's instruction with Eve. And it is Adam's authority that The Serpent is pursuing.

Week 39, Day 1

Indeed, has God said...

"You shall not eat from any tree of the garden'?" Unlike Eve, The Serpent, the covering cherub, knew precisely what God had said to Adam. But he gives the impression that he didn't know. A few sayings provide you with a perspective on this encounter. If Satan were honest, he would say of himself, "Everything I say is a lie, including what I just said." You would say of Satan, "If his lips are moving, he is lying." Jesus says to those who did not believe Him in John 8:44, "You are of your father, the devil, and you want to do the desires of your father. He was a murderer from the beginning and does not stand in the truth because there is no truth in him. Whenever he speaks a lie, he speaks from his own nature, for he is a liar and the father of lies." Lies never lead to truth. When you lie, you join the work of Satan in the world. That is why it is essential always to speak the truth, no matter what.

Week 39, Day 2

The Woman said to the serpent...

One of the beautiful things about reading is the pictures the authors paint in your imagination. Unfortunately, many times in the Bible, you are left with just the facts. There are no grand descriptions of the moment. What was the setting? How did The Serpent look? Was Eve afraid, suspicious, or comfortable? How did their voices sound? What did the garden look like? So today, set your imagination free. Describe the scene in detail with paints, written word, video, or audio recording. Remember what you know of the creation, the Serpent's motives, and the situation in which Eve finds herself. This project may take a few days.

Week 39, Day 3

The Woman said to the serpent…

I hope you found it helpful to imagine what it was like for Eve to speak to The Serpent. When you explore the Bible's events, the Holy Spirit reveals more truths for you to understand, hopefully, that occurred for you. Now with high confidence, Eve answers the Serpent's question. Remember, it is so imperative that you remind each other of what God's word says. The New Testament calls this making a disciple. It is one of our primary tasks in your service of the Lord. The Woman and Adam probably had discussed the commandment of the Lord many times, not knowing that it would one day come into question. This point is true of your faith also. It is of tremendous importance that you are continually discussing your faith with other believers. Your faith will be questioned one day, and you must be ready to answer with God's word. Take time to read about Jesus' faith as He was tempted by the same Serpent in Matthew chapter four. How did Jesus answer the Devil's questions?

Week 39, Day 4

The Woman said to the serpent...

Compare the answer the Woman gave The Serpent and the commandment God gave Adam. Here is what Eve said. "From the fruit of the trees of the garden you may eat; but from the fruit of the tree which is in the middle of the garden, you shall not eat from it or touch it, or you will die." (Genesis 3:2-3) Here is what God told Adam. "From any tree of the garden you may eat freely; but from the tree of the knowledge of good and evil you shall not eat, for in the day that you eat from it you will surely die." (Genesis 2:16-17) What is similar? What is different?

Week 39, Day 5

The Woman said to the serpent…

What did you find when you compared the two verses? What was similar? They both said that she could eat the fruit of the trees of the garden. They both said there was a particular tree she could not eat. Also, she would die if she ate that specific fruit. What was different? Eve described the tree by location rather than by its name. God called it the tree of knowledge of good and evil. Also, the Woman adds that she was not even to touch the fruit. If someone says to you the tree in your front yard or the oak tree at your house, are they saying the same thing or something different? If you say to someone, "Don't eat the cookies," or say, "Don't eat the cookies, don't you even touch them," are you saying the same thing? Knowing precisely what God's word says is essential for us as believers. You must not only know what God said but also understand what God intended for us to do or not do. Did the Woman understand what God said by conveying that truth in her statement, or was she confused and incorrect in what she said?

Week 39, Day 6

The Woman said to the serpent...

Read James 1:2-4. A trial is when your faith in what God tells us is tested. The passage says that remaining faithful to God's word will ultimately make us perfect and complete. The Woman's faith in what Adam has told her God said is about to be tested. Will she believe in God or The Serpent? What are the possible dangers for Eve? First, it could be that she did not know God's command. Possibly she did not understand the importance of obedience. Another option is that she could be deceived into thinking God's word was invalid. Or, finally, she could give in to the desire to have something God said was not good for her. Every day you are in the same place as the Woman. Your faith is tested continuously. The big question is, will you remain faithful to God's word?

Week 40, Day 1

You surely will not die!

The Serpent said, "You surely will not die!" God said, "You will surely die." Who is telling the truth? Time to put yourself in the story. You are the Woman. As far as you know, you will decide for the first time in your life. Who should you believe? The God, who, according to Adam, created you, placed you in the garden, and provided for your needs, or The Serpent, who is the covering Cherub and dwells in the very presence of God? Do you believe Adam or The Serpent? You did not see God form the animals as Adam had. Up to this point, nothing has died. Now you have two options: Believe by faith what was told you by Adam, or make a logical decision based on what you can see. It is the same decision that you will make throughout your life. "Now, faith is the assurance of things hoped for, the conviction of things not seen." (Hebrews 11:1)

Week 40, Day 2

For God knows…

Thus begins the great deception that brings about the fall of man. Most parents have been faithful in telling their children the truth about life. They warn their children over and over again about things that are not good for them, something that would harm them or worse. But in your life, there will be people who will challenge those warnings. They will say, "Parents are crazy. They don't know what they are talking about. They just don't want you to have any fun. Parents know if you tried it, you would really like it." Suddenly a child's mind begins to think, "Is there something my parents aren't telling me? Have they hidden some truth from me?" Deception grows out of the seed of doubt. Deception slips into a person's thoughts when there is doubt in authority. The Woman begins to think, "Did God really tell Adam the whole story?"

Week 40, Day 3

For God knows...

In life, logic can be a great friend. It can keep you from making numerous mistakes. You are often tempted to think something is possible, but logic lets you know it is impossible. For example, many people spend a lot of money buying government-operated education lottery tickets thinking they will get rich. But what does logic tell you? During the recent lottery, 132 million tickets were sold for $2 each. Over $264 million was collected. Logic would say several things to you. First, your chances of winning are slim, 1 in 292,201,338 winning combinations. Second, the government is the only one getting rich. They collected $264 million, but the winner only received $148 million, of which that person would pay the government $74 million in taxes. So the government took 190 million dollars by deceiving people into thinking they would get rich without working. Finally, only 1/3 of the funds collected actually go to education. That would be around $88 million. The rest goes to those who run the lottery. So, what does logic tell us about gambling? It is not very intelligent! But why do people keep wasting their family's money? Because they believe the deception rather than the truth. The Woman is about to buy the first "lottery ticket."

Week 40, Day 4

For God knows…

The Serpent now lays out his argument for why what God told Adam is invalid. "For God knows." The first reason is that God has not told you the whole truth. There are things God knows that if you knew them, it would change what you thought was right. The second reason is "that in the day you eat from it, your eyes will be opened." By eating the fruit, you will obtain the knowledge you don't have now. The third thing is that instead of dying, you will actually "be like God." You will know what He knows. Even more than that, you won't need Him to tell you what is good and evil. In fact, you will make your own decisions about what to do and not do because you will be like Him, "knowing good from evil." You will become an independent being. Able to do what you think best. You'll indeed be free, and God knows this. Just try it and see if I'm not telling you the truth. Your life will be better than before. So who would you believe? Adam, who told you what God said? Or would you believe the Serpent who told you what God knew?

Week 40, Day 5

For God knows…

Most folks are familiar with the story of Jack and the Beanstalk. It was first published in 1734. But the version most often seen was rewritten by Joseph Jacobs in English Fairy Tales (1890). Indeed, you remember the storyline of a poor son who trades the family cow, the family's last hope, for a few magical beans. Imagine how crushing it was to his mother when she realized that somehow a man had gotten her son to trade a cow for a few beans. What was Jack supposed to do? Sell the cow and bring back "seed to plant a good crop." What did Jack do? He traded the cow for a few beans. Did he return with seed to plant? Absolutely not. When you look at the story, there is no doubt of what happened, but why did it happen? Did he disobey his mother, or did the old man deceive him? Not every mistake in life is a result of disobedience. Sometimes deception plays a considerable role.

Week 40, Day 6

For God knows...

As you have learned most of the time, logic is your friend. The Woman is about to use her logic based on what The Serpent has told her. She observes that the fruit of the tree was good for food. Yet, it isn't clear how she knew that. Possibly animals had eaten of it and suffered no ill effects. Her eyes saw the fruit was delightful. The word in Hebrew means that the fruit created a desire in her. Have you ever smelled good food cooking and just had to have some? That is the word. It produced an overwhelming desire in her to have it. Then it says it was desirable to make one wise. The word desirable means it would be a pleasure. From what The Serpent had revealed and what she had personally observed, her logic told her it would be pleasing to have what the fruit offered. What is the error in Eve's logic?

Week 41, Day 1

...she took from its fruit and ate...

There comes a turning point in every story. It is the moment when everything changes. For the apostle Paul, it was meeting the Lord on the road to Damascus. For Moses, it was meeting God at the burning bush. For Judas, it was the moment he met with the Jewish leaders to betray Christ. For almost everyone there is a moment that changes everything from that point forward. Sometimes that moment is the best thing that could ever happen, and sometimes it is the worst. Often the turning point in a person's life comes from circumstances beyond their control, like an accident or an action started by someone else. But often, like this one for the Woman, they come from our own decisions. That is why being sure of what you believe is so important. If she had truly understood and acted accordingly to what Adam told her, how different would this moment have been? In your life, you will make decisions that will significantly affect you and those you love. Will you trust in your reasoning or the very words of God? Memorize Proverbs 3:5-6.

Week 41, Day 2

...she took from its fruit and ate...

Do you remember what the goal of The Serpent was? Sometimes you can get lost in the circumstances and miss the point. Do you remember the first time you saw a great magician make something disappear? No way the item can vanish, people watching his every move, and not a hiding place in sight. Then a curtain was drawn around. With a quick word from the magician, the curtain drops to reveal the item has disappeared. Completely vanished before your eyes. Did the magician make it vanish supernaturally? No, it was a trick, a deception. Some who are watching just enjoyed the illusion. Others thought endlessly, "How did he do that?" But for that particular person, it birthed in them a desire to be like one of the great magicians. What was the Serpent's goal? To get the Woman to eat the forbidden fruit? No, his goal was to usurp the authority over the creation that God had given Adam. So why do you think he came to Eve first?

Week 41, Day 3

…she gave also to her husband…

What was the moment like? Was the fruit as good as she expected? Did she suddenly have the knowledge she thought she would obtain? The Bible doesn't tell us what the Woman experienced at this point. Instead, it reveals the most shocking revelation in all of Scripture. "And she gave also to her husband WITH her." Adam was there the whole time. Adam heard what The Serpent said and saw how the Woman responded to the fruit. But he said absolutely NOTHING! The Man knew precisely what God had said. He knew she would die if she ate the fruit. But said nothing to refute The Serpent. Adam uttered absolutely nothing to correct the Woman. Did nothing to stop her from taking the fruit. What was his responsibility? What should he have done? Why didn't he act? What is your responsibility when you see those around you choosing things that are not God's best for them?

Week 41, Day 4

…and he ate.

There are moments when people say, "This event will change the world forever." They are usually overstating the event for emphasis. Though the episode may have changed the course of history in the long run, it often falls in with similar events. Many of these are lost in history and with limited impact. But that is not the case with the phrase you read today. "And he ate." This one phrase literally changed the course of all creation. This action, taken by Adam, affected every person in a highly negative way and all creation from that moment forward. His decision to eat the forbidden fruit unleashed a horrifying evil into God's perfect creation. No other action by a person in history, no matter how devastating, has ever affected the world like this one event. This deed should constantly remind you that your decisions and subsequent actions don't just affect you. Choices have consequences that those around you must live with. Adam never thought that what he did thousands of years ago would release a plague that would continue to affect the creation forever, but it did.

Week 41, Day 5

...and he ate.

So why do you think Adam and the Woman ate of the fruit? The quick answer is disobedience to God's command. God told them not to eat off the tree, and they did. End of the story. But what prompted them to think this was a good idea? For the answer, you need the rest of the Bible. God's word is complete, but it doesn't always tell the whole story in one place. 1 Timothy 2:14 says, "And it was not Adam who was deceived, but the Woman being deceived, fell into transgression." The Woman was deceived and therefore fell into disobedience to God's command. You have learned that deception is the work of the Evil One, Satan. He is continually trying to deceive God's people into disobeying The Lord. Unfortunately, certain people are either wrong in what they teach or intentionally trying to mislead others for personal gain. That is why you must know God's word and act accordingly. There is a saying, "Ignorance of the law is no excuse." Even though the Woman was deceived, she was not innocent. The Bible says she fell into transgression.

Week 41, Day 6

…and he ate.

But what about Adam? You just read that he was not deceived. The Serpent had not tricked him at all. He was well aware of what he had done. So what was going on in Adam that made him eat the forbidden fruit? James 1:14-15 says, "But each one is tempted when he is carried away and enticed by his own lust. Then when lust has conceived, it gives birth to sin; and when sin is accomplished, it brings forth death." The temptation is not sinning. The Bible says in Hebrews 4:15 that our Lord Jesus was tempted in all ways, just like us. When Adam was tempted, he became enticed by his own lust to be like God. The Serpent shared the possibility, but it was Adam's lust that began to convince him that he could be like God. When his desire convinced him that it was possible, it took control of his actions, and the result was sin. The sin in The Serpent entered Adam because he gave in to the lust generated by the temptation. That is why Jesus teaches us to pray, "Lead us not into temptation." It is so important to remember that avoiding sin begins with handling temptation.

Week 42, Day 1

...and he ate.

"Therefore, just as through one man sin entered into the world, and death through sin, and so death spread to all men, because all sinned." (Romans 5:12). The iniquity that drove The Serpent to rebel against God now entered the creation through Adam. It was Adam's sin that unleashed death in the world. "The thief comes only to steal and kill and destroy;" (John 10:10). The Serpent is the thief. His goal was to steal the authority of Adam. By Adam's choice to believe the lie and give in to his own lust, he gave Satan the authority. Just as Esau gave up his birthright for a bowl of lentil stew, Adam gave Satan his authority in the world for forbidden fruit. Satan did not have to harm Adam. He just had to present a temptation that Adam did not resist and allowed sin to enter. Adam had no clue what his actions would bring upon the whole world. Read Luke 4:5-7. Satan is still in the deception business. Remember what James 4:7 says, "Submit therefore to God. Resist the devil, and he will flee from you."

Week 42, Day 2

…and he ate.

Take time to read the temptation of Christ in Luke 4:1-13. Look specifically at verses 5 and 6. Satan takes Jesus and shows Him all the kingdoms of the world in one moment in time. Then the Devil says, "I will give You this domain and its glory; for it has been handed over to me." As you know, the New Testament was originally written in Greek. The Greek language is very descriptive. Many Greek words are the basis for our English words. The word translated as "handed over to me" is the word *paradidomai*. The picture of the word is the transfer of something from one person to another. The way the verb is written indicates a transfer that happened in the past but is still in effect. Adam handed over the authority God had given him when Adam believed the Devil rather than God. Now Satan would be the ruler, but not the owner of this world.

Week 42, Day 3

…and he ate.

Three times in the Gospel of John, Jesus addresses the subject of who is in authority in the world. Read John 12:31, 14:30, 16:11, and the surrounding verses. Each time he refers to the ruler of this world, it is not Him but Satan. Jesus also references seeing Satan fall and being judged. The good news is that Jesus, through His faithfulness, eventually will take authority from Satan. But it does not correct all the damage Adam has done by his unfaithfulness. Satan still maintains an influence in the creation through the continued sin of all humanity. However, his power over humanity is limited to those who allow him to control their lives. There is freedom in the Lord Jesus.

Week 42, Day 4

...and he ate.

Adam's failure to obey God is the source of humanity's separation from God. This separation is the Fall of humankind. All the ills of this world. All the sin that plagues all humanity. All the pain of living in a fallen world is traced back to this moment in time. Adam's failure to obey God affects every person and everything that has ever existed in the creation. Think of sin as a contagious disease. When Adam gave in to the temptation to be like God, Satan's sin disease came to him. As the father of all humankind, it spread to all people. All humanity is born in sin. But more importantly, all of humanity has given in to sin by their own choice. The Bible says this in Romans 3:23, "For ALL have sinned and come short of the glory of God." Though you would like to blame Adam for all our problems, the truth is you willingly continue the sin disease yourself. It is the reason all humanity needs a Savior.

Week 42, Day 5

Then the eyes of both of them were opened…

Get a blindfold and a set of earplugs. Now put them on. Have someone drive you to a place you have never been to before. Stand for a few moments and get settled. Then describe what you are sensing. Take off your blindfold and remove your earplugs. Were you where you thought you were? What was it like to see it for the first time? Or to hear the sounds? Now imagine what it was like for Adam and the Woman. Read Genesis 2:25. Now read Genesis 3:7. What difference had sin made in their lives?

Week 42, Day 6

...And they knew that they were naked...

Compare two verses, Genesis 2:25 and Genesis 3:7. What do you see that is similar, and what do you see is different? In 2:25, they were naked but were not ashamed. In verse 3:7, they were naked, and they were ashamed. However, the words used for naked in the two verses are different. In 2:25, the word would be the same as you think of nudity. But in 3:7, the term is best translated as exposed or uncovered. Remember that to be in the presence of the Lord God; they had to be enclothed in light. (Week 14, Day 3) But once sin entered their lives, the light was gone. They saw themselves uncovered, exposed, not enclothed in light. Sin transformed how they appeared and how they felt about their appearance. Innocence lost is the immediate consequence of sin.

Week 43, Day 1

...they sewed fig leaves together...

Sin makes you do strange things. Go to a garden shop and see what fig leaves look like, or search the internet for fig leaves. Now imagine how you would link together those leaves to cover yourself. Then go home and draw a picture of what you think they looked like covered in fig leaves. How do you think they looked? Did they look like they had good sense? Did it really hide their shame? Who or what were they covering themselves from? The first thing you learn about sin is that it brings shame. You want to hide from everyone. Attempts to hide shame only make you look more guilty. Years ago, a singing group, The Cathedrals, wrote a song. You can look it up on YouTube. Here are the lyrics, "Sin will take you farther than you wanna go, Slowly but wholly taking control, Sin will leave you longer than you wanna stay, Sin will cost you far more than you wanna pay...".

Week 43, Day 2

…and made themselves loin coverings.

You have probably heard this saying, "Clothing makes the man." If that is true, what does that make Adam? The first clothes were fig leaves. Obviously, there was not a great deal of thought that went into the first designer outfits. The disgrace that Adam and the Woman felt led them to attempt to cover their shame. Based on this passage, rabbis apply this proverb: "If you acted disgracefully, take a thread and sew." This saying teaches every person is responsible for their actions and that the consequences of immoral behavior are accompanied by physical exertion. Adam and the Woman's sin also brought physical labor to the world, for from then on, man would have to toil to produce crops to eat.

Week 43, Day 3

They heard the sound…

What happens next in the story of creation is quite remarkable. "They heard the sound of the LORD God walking in the garden in the cool of the day." What do you think that sounded like? Did God actually walk in the garden like a person? Many times in the Old Testament, God appears in a physical form. When this happens, it is called a theophany. That's a big word that, in Greek, means to "show God." In this phrase, "the cool" means spirit or wind. God could have appeared as the sound of the wind or the third person of the Trinity, the Holy Spirit. But does the Spirit walk? When God walks on the earth, what does He look like? John 14:9 tells us that Jesus said to Philip, "He who has seen Me has seen the Father." So who do you think was walking in the garden?

Week 43, Day 4

The man and wife hid themselves…

The presence of good and evil knowledge in a person's life is their conscience. Your conscience is the feeling that either sends a warning or approval of what you have done or will do. It makes you feel proud when you make the right decision and ashamed when you make a terrible decision. Adam and the Woman demonstrated their conscience when they hid from the presence of God. They were ashamed of what they had done. Take time to look up the word barometer. What does it do? It senses the pressure in the atmosphere. Notice the range it measures in inches of mercury, 27.5 to 31.5. All the atmospheric pressures ever registered in history fall within 4 inches of measurement. Even a slight change makes a tremendous difference in the weather. That is the way it is with our conscience. Even a subtle move toward evil leads to a very different result. That is why you read the Bible daily. You must continuously fine-tune your conscience to God's word.

Week 43, Day 5

...from the presence of the Lord...

What happens when you have done something wrong and someone finds out? Do you want to see them? Do you want to hear what they have to say? Do you want them to look at you? No. Why not? Are you afraid of them or ashamed of what you have done? Shame is what sin does to you. It makes you fearful of the ones who love you more than anyone else. Who loved Adam more than anyone else? Yet he hides from His Creator. When a child sins, this is what shame says, "I've just made a huge mistake. Don't tell my parents". Here is what love says, "I've just made a huge mistake. I need to tell my parents." Sin will always try to separate you from those that love you most.

Week 43, Day 6

Where are you?

What is a rhetorical question? It is a question asked to create a dramatic effect or make a point rather than an answer. In Genesis 3:9, God asks the first question ever asked, which is rhetorical. God knows exactly where Adam is physically located. He also knows what Adam has done. More importantly, He knows why Adam has committed this dreadful act. The question is asked to make a point. God wants Adam to realize where he is in his relationship with the Lord. God asks questions like this many times in the Bible to make people think and ultimately repent. The question God asks you today is, "Where are you?" Walking with God or hiding in the trees.

Week 44, Day 1

I heard the sound of You walking in the garden…

How often do you think Adam heard the Lord walking in the garden? How do you think he had reacted before this time? There was once a little boy. When his Dad came home from work each day, he would hear him coming up the walk and run out to greet him. His father would pick him up on his shoulders and carry him into the house. They would laugh when Dad bent down to get in the door. It was the best time of the day. But there were days when the son had not behaved well. The sound of his father coming up the walk did not produce joy but fear. He dreaded the very moment that previously had brought him such pleasure. He wanted to hide. What caused the difference in the two moments? Was it the sound he heard, was it fear of his father who loved him, was it shame, or was it something different? Why did Adam behave the way he did?

Week 44, Day 2

...and I was afraid because I was naked...

The fight-or-flight response (also called hyperarousal or the acute stress response) is a physiological reaction that occurs in response to a perceived harmful event, attack, or threat to survival. (Wikipedia, Fight or Flight Response) Fear is what brings this response to an action. Because you fear, you either fight it or run and hide. It is generally thought that courage is to face your fear, and cowardice is hiding from it. When your sin causes fear, you either confront and confess it or flee and deny it. How different would life be if Adam had confronted his sin and confessed instead of hiding? How different would your life be if you faced your sin and admitted it rather than having hidden what you had done? God always seeks and desires confession. 1 John 1:9 says, "If you confess your sins, He is faithful and righteous to forgive us our sins and cleanse us from all unrighteousness."

Week 44, Day 3

…so I hid myself…

Do you notice the pattern sin created in Adam? When he became aware (I heard the sound), he became afraid and ashamed (I was naked), then he hid. This behavior is the pattern of sin in our lives. Aware of our sin, fearful of the consequences of sin, and ashamed of the evil committed. If the sound of those that love you produces fear, you could be in sin. If you are ashamed of something you have done, you could be in sin. If you hide what you have done, you could sin. These actions: fear, shame, and hiding, are all signs you need to check yourself. You need to be honest with yourself and God. What produced in your life fear, shame, and deceit? When you find out what it is, you can confess and repent. And with that, restore your relationship with the Lord and others.

Week 44, Day 4

Who told you that you were naked?

What does it mean to have the knowledge of good and evil? Before eating the fruit, the man and woman were innocent. They were naked and unashamed. Now they hide in shame of being exposed. God asks them another rhetorical question. "Who told you that you were naked?" The answer was no one. They knew within themselves because of the knowledge of good and evil. A sinful nature had replaced an innocent nature. No one had to tell them. They knew. The problem was they knew too late. God had told them before the danger of disobedience, but now they knew. So God gave His people the Ten Commandments to warn them of disobedience. But as you have learned by experience, sin can trump knowledge. Knowledge is no defense against wickedness. Only obedience brings righteousness.

Week 44, Day 5

Who told you that you were naked?

It may seem impossible for you today to feel what Adam and the Woman thought at that moment. Not just the shame but the loss. Have you ever let someone down in a crucial moment? Your disappointment is enough, but now try to imagine if you had never had that feeling of loss. There are beautiful moments when a person who has been deaf hears for the first time. Or a person who has been crippled by accident can walk again. But this moment goes the opposite way. Life had been perfect for the first humans. Everything had been entirely prepared for them. But suddenly, negative emotions appear. The relationship that was so good has now soured. That same pain of sin comes to all of Adam's descendants when they realize they are without hope in a lost and fallen world.

Week 44, Day 6

Have you eaten from the tree of which I commanded you not to eat?

God continues to ask questions to which He already knows the answer. Is it to shame Adam and the Woman more? Is it to remind them of their unfaithfulness? Is it to say, "I told you so"? No, it is love. Real love is founded in truth. Paul says, "Love rejoices in the truth." Being honest, even in a shameful situation, removes the sting of sin. Confession of wrongdoing is the first step in the process of forgiveness. It is telling the truth about what you have done. Loving someone who has done something wrong begins with bringing them to realize what they have done. When they can confess what they have done, forgiveness can be given. Then restoration of the relationship can begin. You must surround yourself with people who love you enough to ask tough questions. What happens if a person cannot confess?

Week 45, Day 1

The man said…

Have you ever had someone tell you the truth to deceive you? You're saying, "How can the truth be used as deception?" Read Genesis 3:12. What does Adam say? "The Woman you gave me." Did God give Adam the Woman? Yes. "She gave me from the tree." Did she? Yes. Adam is answering God as to why he ate of the tree. The things he said are correct but intended to conceal why he ate the fruit. Adam says God was responsible for what happened because God gave him the Woman. He uses what truly happened to shift the blame to God and the Woman. Have you ever done that? It might sound like this, "Everybody else was doing it." Or "I didn't do it first." You are always responsible for your actions. The truth must never be twisted to deceive.

Week 45, Day 2

…she gave me from the tree…

Have you ever heard the term "throwing someone under the bus"? It means to cause someone else to suffer to save oneself or gain personal advantage. Say you are doing something wrong with another person. When questioned, you say it was the other person's idea or did it first. This is what Adam has done to the Woman. The big question is, why would he do this? Here is the first picture of what the Bible later calls the flesh. The flesh is how you attempt to manage the pains of life without God. Adam knows he has disappointed God, and it hurts. To avoid the pain, he selfishly blames the Woman. Essentially, he says it was not his fault, and God should not be disappointed in Adam. Unfortunately, because of Adam's sin, all have "sinful flesh" at work in humanity, trying to manage the pain of living in a fallen world. When someone hurts you or is disobedient, how do you try to keep from hurting? Do you ever throw others under the bus?

Week 45, Day 3

The serpent deceived me…

Read Genesis 3:12-13. How different are the responses of Adam and the Woman? Adam immediately blamed others for his wrongdoing. But how did the Woman respond? Did she lash out at Adam for placing the blame on her? Did she, like Adam, try to blame God? Did she complain about the commandment being too hard or unreasonable? When asked what she had done, what was her answer? She told the truth. The Serpent had deceived her. She had been tricked into doing what was wrong. You only have the words she said. You don't know how she said it. People can tell the truth in defiance or confession. It could be she didn't care; she just knew she had done it wrong. Or she could have been very broken by her failure. You don't know. But what you do know is she answered truthfully when Adam did not. Reread Romans 5:12. "Through one man sin entered into the world."

Week 45, Day 4

…and I ate.

Consequences are the results of our actions. It is what happens as a result of something a person has done. The word is almost always used in a negative sense. There is an expected adverse consequence when you do something that is not God's best for you. God gives you His word to guide what is best for you. When you follow His direction, the adverse effects are minimized. Even with confessing your wrongdoing, negative consequences are likely to occur. Adam and the Woman failed to obey the desires of the Lord. What do you think they thought would happen? Do you think they felt that everyone who ever lived on the earth would suffer because of what they did? Did they believe every aspect of God's perfect creation would be ruined? From this story, you can see that your actions create consequences not limited to just you. They can and do affect others. You make decisions for others, not just yourself, every time you decide. You don't live in isolation. It certainly places obedience to God's word as the top priority for your life.

Week 45, Day 5

The Lord God said…

There once were two brothers, James and John. Like brothers everywhere, they eventually got in trouble for breaking things while wrestling in the house. Both received a lecture on obedience. But James was sent outdoors, while John was given time out sitting facing the corner. A neighbor, noticing the strange way of discipline, asked, "Why do you punish them differently?" The parents responded, "Because they are each unique. James is an indoor child. John is an outdoor child." Discipline must fit not just the offense but also the person. When God's judgment came, it was unique to all parties, the Serpent, The Woman, and Adam. Each received a curse that constantly reminded them of their sin but was also uniquely designed for them.

Week 45, Day 6

The Lord God said…

Passing a harsh judgment on anyone is a painful event. Every judge that sits in court feels the weight of the decision. Every parent feels the anguish that is associated with carrying out chastisement. And indeed, every child feels the pain of the reprimand. Yet, there seems to be a greater empathy for the one who receives the punishment. There is a tendency to perceive the one being punished deserves more thought. After all, they will have to live with the consequences of their actions. But what about those who have been offended? Adam and the Woman are certainly tragic figures in the story. A paradise that was once theirs is about to be lost. But what about God? God created two perfect beings with whom He could have a relationship. But now He is rejected by the very people He made. The loss for God is far more significant. It would be best to keep that in mind when sin leads you to be disobedient.

Week 46, Day 1

The Lord God said to the serpent…

The Serpent, the covering cherub. The one who had dwelled in the very presence of God until iniquity was found in him. The one who brought sin into the creation through deception and temptation. Now faces God in judgment. He has accomplished all he wanted by usurping Adam's authority in creation. But soon, the consequences of his deception would come. Would it be banishment, eternal torment, or complete destruction? Surprisingly none of the above. Despite the apparent defeat, God's plan for His creation is still working. This should be a great reminder to you. Nothing is going as you planned, all seems lost, and it seems hopeless, but God is still working. His plan for your life is still intact. God wastes nothing. Even pain, suffering, or defeat are all used by Him to complete His design for your life.

Week 46, Day 2

The Lord God said to the serpent…

A curse is a solemn expression intended to invoke a supernatural capacity to inflict damage or punishment on someone or something. Do you remember what you found about the Serpent's sin? It was the sin of pride. He wanted to set his throne over God's throne. What is the opposite of pride? Right, humiliation. So what would you do if you wanted to punish or hurt someone full of pride? Humiliate them. That's what God does to the covering cherub. The one who used to dwell in the very presence of God is now cursed with being forced to be lower than the animals God created. The Serpent, known also as the Covering Cherubim, would forever be considered the lowest of God's created beings. The one who stood in the presence of glory was now condemned to crawl in the dust of the earth. No longer would his beauty be on display, only his humiliation. To this day, the Serpent, Satan, is reviled and scorned by all the creation.

Week 46, Day 3

And I will put enmity...

But the curse is not limited to just humiliation. The condemnation of the opposition joins it. The role of the Serpent throughout history would be one of contending with humanity. Read Genesis 3:15. God placed an enmity between the Serpent and the Woman, the state or feeling of being actively opposed or hostile to someone or something. Forever there would be a war between the descendant of the Woman and the Serpent. The curse divides humankind into these two groups. There is no in-between, only one or the other. You are either of The Serpent or the Woman with eternal opposition to one another. The question must be, how do I know which group I belong to? Is there a way to change sides?!?

Week 46, Day 4

He shall bruise you on the head...

Many times you think you understand something. The answer seems so obvious. But when you dig deeper, there is more to the story. Such is the curse given to the Serpent. It seems reasonably clear that the Serpent has been humiliated and will be opposed by the Woman's what you think are her descendants—end of story. But wait, there is more. "He shall bruise you on the head, And you shall bruise him on the heel." Generally, you see the word "seed" as plural descendants. But this phrase says he, singular. The word bruise has an expansive meaning, anywhere from an injury to crush. But the point here is very significant. God says that a male, from the seed of the Woman, not of Adam, will come and inflict great harm on (the head) of the Serpent. And the Serpent will harm (the heel) of Him. Can you guess who this One is, born solely of the Woman, not Man? Though still far off, God's plan to save humanity begins to take shape here.

Week 46, Day 5

He shall bruise you on the head…

You learned much earlier in your study there is a physical creation you can see and a spiritual creation that you do not see. Both are very real, and both are affected dramatically by the curses. The humiliation of the Serpent ultimately will result in the shame of Satan being cast out of heaven. Many angels in the spiritual world follow the leadership of Satan and rebel against God. This spiritual warfare spills over into the physical world, as you see in this story. That is why you must understand that curses are not just manifested physically. Everything that happens in what you can see affects what you do not see. And everything that happens in the spiritual affects the physical. Know that when you stand for the Lord in the face of opposition in this world, it affects mightily what is occurring in the spiritual realm. Your prayer must be that God's will be done on earth (physical) as in heaven (spiritual).

Week 46, Day 6

To the woman He said…

Read Genesis 1:28. What was the first command God gave the Man and Woman He created? Be fruitful and multiply and fill the earth. As you remember from your earlier study, the creation is designed to reproduce itself. Humanity would reproduce itself by giving birth to children. This was the gift of God to humankind. "Behold, children are a gift of the LORD, The fruit of the womb is a reward." (Psalms 127:3). As a consequence of disobedience, the first portion of the curse says that the Woman's pain would be multiplied in childbirth. The Bible doesn't tell you how much pain would have been in delivery from the beginning, but whatever pain there was is now increased. Interestingly, the word multiply is the same in Genesis 1:28 and 3:16. God's blessing of multiplying at the beginning of creation now becomes the curse of painfully birthing a child in the Fall of humanity.

Week 47, Day 1

Yet your desire…

As you discovered earlier in your studies, the foundation of human relationships is the family. The family begins with the union of a husband and wife in marriage. The marriage relationship is the key then to the well-being of all humanity. When that relationship is strong, the family is healthy, and, in turn, society is secure. Therefore, anything that intentionally disrupts the unity of marriage would be considered a curse. This brings us to the second half of God's curse on the Woman. The Fall of humankind didn't just affect the relationship with God. It also created a divide in the marriage relationship. One simple phrase, "Yet your desire will be for your husband, and he will rule over you," would lead to the most significant conflicts marriages would endure forever.

Week 47, Day 2

…will be for your husband…

Try this experiment. Get a small jar and fill it half full of water. Find some cooking oil. Fill the rest of the jar with cooking oil. Put the lid on the jar and shake it for 30 seconds. Place it on the table and let it sit for an hour. Now go back and observe what has happened. Did the water and oil mix together to make a solution? Or did the oil and water separate? The water molecules attract each other, and the oil molecules stick together. That causes oil and water to form two distinct layers. Water molecules pack closer together, sinking to the bottom and leaving oil on top of the water. Because of their natural properties, water and oil can never unify and become one. Now read Genesis 2:24. How are this experiment and the verse related?

Week 47, Day 3

...and he will...

Remember the definition of a curse? It is a solemn expression intended to invoke a supernatural capacity to inflict damage or punishment on someone or something. In Genesis 2:24, what was the ultimate goal of marriage? For the two to become one. What would you do if you wanted to inflict harm or punishment on marriage? You would make it difficult or impossible for the two to become one or unified. What makes it impossible for oil and water to become unified? Their natural properties. What they are made of. Therefore, the curse would have to alter the natural tendency for a man and woman to become one. The curse would then cause the conflict to occur naturally. What happens when one person is made the leader, but the other is more capable of leading? Unity or conflict?

Week 47, Day 4

...rule over you.

English translations fail to adequately convey the concepts of the Hebrew language in this verse. "Yet your desire will be for your husband, and he will rule over you." Let's look at the role of the husband in the marriage. The word rule is marshal, and it means to govern. It is used in Chapter 1:18 as descriptive of the sun and the day. The sun governs the day. The day starts when the sun rises and ends when the sun sets. The sun doesn't own the day; it makes the day possible. The word is also used of those who govern people. The governor doesn't own the people but is accountable for making people's lives possible. The idea of ruling here is not dominating or subduing. It is a responsibility. The husband is responsible for the wife and, ultimately, the family. His role is to ensure his wife's life is all it should be. He must have the authority to make the decisions for her well-being. In other words, he must lead her to the best life possible. However, this is only possible when she follows his lead.

Week 47, Day 5

...rule over you.

Have you ever tried to get someone to do something they didn't want to do? This is especially true when they ultimately want to get you to do what they want. If you have played out this scenario, you know what the curse does to the marriage relationship. The first part of the curse says, "Yet your desire (the Woman) will be for your husband." On the surface, this sounds sweet. Certainly, a loving wife would desire her husband. But that's not the word here. It is only used twice in the Bible. The other time gives us a better picture of the word's meaning. It occurs in Genesis 4:7 "If you do well, will not your countenance be lifted up? And if you do not do well, sin is crouching at the door; and its desire is for you, but you must master it." The last phrase is the key to understanding the curse. God says to Cain, "Sin desires (same word) to control you, but you must rule (same word as used of Adam's role) over sin." When you transfer this meaning to the curse, it says that the Woman will desire to control Adam, but he is the one who is responsible for leading. Now can you see how the curse affects marriages forever? The one who follows the leadership actually wants to control the one who is supposed to lead. How hard will it be to have unity?

Week 47, Day 6

Love and Respect

The Bible has some great advice that will solve this issue for you. Look at Ephesians 5:33 "Nevertheless, each individual among you also is to love his own wife even as himself, and the wife must see to it that she respects her husband." God ordained a solution to the curse. It is straightforward and easy to remember. Husband love your wife as yourself, and wife respect your husband. Now, of course, that is easier said than done. But in the words of the great theologian, Mr. Fred Rogers, "If it can be said, it can be managed." What has been shared here will be the most important thing you can possibly know about the marriage relationship. If you only learn and practice this lesson, you will be most blessed.

Week 48, Day 1

Love and Respect

Next to your relationship with the Lord Jesus, marriage is the most important relationship a person can have. Even more significant than the parent-child relationship. Therefore, it is paramount that you understand how the curse affects how husbands and wives relate to one another. Whether a couple is a follower of Christ or not, the curse is present in their marriage. How they manage this determines God's best for them. A wise man once said you could fix ANYTHING with duct tape and a coat hanger. Using these items rather than returning the equipment to how it was designed to operate, you make do with less than the best. It may serve in the short run but it is not the best solution. Many couples make a marriage work even without love and respect. But that's not God's best for you. You know the truth, and your marriage deserves God's best.

Week 48, Day 2

Love and Respect

Why something happens is just as important as what happens. It is called motive, the reason you do something. Why you do things is very important to God. 1 Samuel 16:7 says, "Do not look at his appearance or at the height of his stature, because I have rejected him; for God sees not as man sees, for man looks at the outward appearance, but the LORD looks at the heart." God knows your motives because He sees your heart. You can say yes and clean your room, but if you are angry because Mom tells you to do it, you have a heart problem. Your wrong motive ruins your efforts. Your motivation must be pure for the action to be pure. What does Genesis 3:17 say was Adam's motive? He listened and obeyed (the meaning of the word *shama* in Hebrew) his wife's voice rather than the voice of God. Adam believed in his heart that it was more important to obey his wife than God. The sin of rebellion began in Adam's heart. His motive was to please his wife rather than God.

Week 48, Day 3

Cursed is the ground because of you...

Out of the ground, God formed man, the beasts, and the vegetation for the garden. In Hebrew, the word ground is from the word Adam. All living things have an association with the ground. Remember, God said it was good. But now, because of Adam's rebellion, God curses the ground from which life came. The land had done nothing wrong. In fact, God used it to produce what He says is good. But now it is cursed. Unfortunately, that's what sin does. It not only affects us, but it also hurts all those things around us. The good creation, not just man, is now fallen. It will never operate in the way it was initially designed. All because of Adam's decision. When you choose to sin, you choose to harm everyone and everything you are associated with. You never hurt only yourself.

Week 48, Day 4

In toil, you will eat of it...

There is a saying, "Choose a job you love, and you will never have to work a day in your life." This advice is excellent. Everyone has to work. Even if you don't have a job, you must work to provide for yourself and your family. If you are doing what you like, the work is more pleasant, but it is still work. For example, Adam was told to cultivate and keep the garden. Since God provided the trees for food, and the trees grew the fruit, the work would have consisted of picking what you desired. But with the curse, Adam would have to till the soil for his food. The word the Bible uses is pain. In pain, Adam would provide his food. Sin made work more complicated, but it also made it painful—what a contrast from what God desired for humanity.

Week 48, Day 5

Both thorns and thistles it shall grow...

Have you ever noticed that you don't have to plant weeds? Corn doesn't just pop up, beans don't just sprout out of the earth, and tomatoes don't appear in the garden. But weeds sure do. Everything good comes from tilling and planting. Even when you plant your seed and it begins to grow, what must you do in the garden? Right, you have to pull weeds. Because God cursed the ground, it produced "thorns and thistles." No longer would the ground provide good food on its own. Now it automatically creates weeds. Here is another point about sin. It comes naturally. Humanity's nature, like the ground's nature, is to produce sin. Sin comes with no effort, but goodness requires effort.

Week 48, Day 6

Both thorns and thistles it shall grow…

Have you ever gone to visit someone for an extended period? Isn't it amazing how they do things differently from you? Get up, go to bed, and eat at different times. And the food. They don't eat the same things nor even fix meals the same way. It changes everything. Now imagine what the curse does for Adam and the Woman. The food they had just picked off the trees would come from the ground through hard work. Now plants would be their mainstay. Take a moment to make a list of the characteristics of plants in the field. Now create a list of the attributes of the fruit of trees. Which are harder to grow plants or fruit trees? Which are more subject to the weather? Which must be planted more often? Which tastes better? It is evident that the curse altered the lives of humankind, and not for the better.

Week 49, Day 1

By the sweat of your face…

There is nothing like hard work on a hot sunny day. Today take time to build up an excellent sweat. The heat and humidity seem to bond together to make your life miserable. Now imagine the same amount of work in air conditioning. The coolness of the air makes the whole event bearable. But now imagine the same job done without any effort at all. That's the real difference the curse made in the life of Adam and the Woman. But what does that mean for you today? It means every time you feel the sweat on your brow. It reminds you of the original sin. Everybody everywhere has felt the effects of perspiration and the curse of sin. It is the universal plague of all humanity.

Week 49, Day 2

Till you return to the ground...

Have you ever heard the phrase, "Life is hard, and then you die"? A rather heartless phrase. Nonetheless, accurate to the human condition. The curse ensures that life is hard, but even more harshly, it says you will die. The Bible puts it this way in Hebrews 9:27, "And inasmuch as it is appointed for men to die once and after this comes judgment." This truth is bad news for all humanity. The hard work of life is no deterrent to the reality of death. No matter what you accomplish or accumulate will remove the inevitability of death. But there is good news. It is called the gospel, and it says, "For God loved the world in this way, He gave His only begotten Son, that whoever believes in Him will not perish, but have everlasting life." (John 3:16)

Week 49, Day 3

Till you return to the ground…

What is the one thing all humans fear? Death. All people die at some point. No matter where he lives, every person lives with the shadow of death. The ominous feeling that one day you will die. Now imagine Adam and the Woman. They had never seen anything die. For them, it was life eternal. But now, because of their sin and the resultant curse, death enters the world. Not knowing what this death would be like produced a great fear. That anxiety had never been present in their lives. For many people, that terror still exists. The fear is based on the unknown. For you, as a Christian, know it leads to eternal life with our Lord Jesus. But for Adam and the Woman, there was no such hope. Only the knowledge that they would die.

Week 49, Day 4

Because from it you were taken...

When God created humankind, He did not create new elements. Humanity was made from the same components, in different percentages, as the ground. Death, therefore, is described as returning to the earth from which humanity was formed. But death is far more than the body ceasing to function for humans. Unlike other creatures, humanity was designed in the image of God. Like God, human beings are triune, three parts, body, soul, and spirit. In death, the body returns to the earth, not the soul and spirit. Unfortunately, Adam eventually realizes that death will ultimately separate him from his Creator forever. Spiritual death, not the physical, is man's greatest fear.

Week 49, Day 5

And to dust you shall return…

God reveals to Adam that he will return to the ground he was taken from at the end of his life. He would return to his elemental nature. The body that was living would decay to the dust of the earth. Many people ask at funerals, "If Jesus gives us eternal life, why must we die physically?" It does seem like a very fair question. It appears that the curse has more effect than the promise of the gospel message. But that's only because of the human perspective. Read 1 Corinthians 15: 50-57. Did you see the reason the body returns to dust? Flesh and blood cannot inherit the kingdom of God. Although the curse is still in effect, it does not affect your place with the Lord Jesus. (2 Corinthians 5:8)

Week 49, Day 6

Now the man called his wife…

You have learned that naming something or someone indicates authority for that item or person. Unfortunately, in today's culture, you do not see honor in this because of our desire for independence and freedom. So, just as parents name their children in great love, Adam now names his wife Eve. Or did he? In the original language of the Bible, Hebrew, her name is Chavvah or simplified Havah. Generally, Biblical names are transliterated. That means taking the letters in the original language and substituting the new language's letters that sound close to the same. But obviously, this was not the case here. The name Eve is from the Latin translation of the Bible and has remained in our English translations. But technically, Adam did not name the Woman Eve, but Havah.

Week 50, Day 1

...Eve, because she was the mother of all the living.

"What's in a name?" is a quote from William Shakespeare's Romeo and Juliet. It proposes an excellent question concerning the name Havah, translated as Eve. The Bible says she was named this because she was "the mother of all the living." Havah is related to the word in Hebrew for life, *chayah*. But her name carries with it much more than just life. First, it relates to the concept of creation—the creating of life. Secondly, there is completion. God created mankind, not only male but male and female. She is the completion of God's creation. Finally, she expresses what life is, the continued procreation process—the beginning of new life, the mother of all the living. Eve is the creation, completion, and expression of what life is. Apart from the Woman, the man cannot create life. He can only take life (as will be seen later). Only in the Woman is there the capacity to give life.

Week 50, Day 2

The Lord God made garments of skin…

Have you ever watched videos of astronauts walking in space? The vision is spectacular, with the earth's glowing curvature and the intense darkness of space in the background. Their weightless condition allows them to float easily from station to station. They are covered in special spacesuits that will enable them to live and work in a place that otherwise would be harmful. It is what is known as a hostile environment. When Adam and Eve were created, they lived in a perfect environment, the very presence of God. They were enclothed in light as the image of God. But as you learned, that shroud of light disappeared when they disobeyed the Lord. They are about to enter a fallen world, cursed by their sin. Not the paradise they had known. Remember that one of the Principles of Living Holy is that God is a provider. Now comes the time for Him to provide a covering to allow humanity to live in a hostile environment.

Week 50, Day 3

...for Adam and his wife...

The result of the disobedience of Adam was the loss of paradise. Adam and Eve will no longer dwell in the Lord's presence. They are now without the protection of their garment of light. The Bible says at this point, "God made for them garments." What kind of garments would you think God would provide, knowing what they were about to encounter? Most pictures created for history books depict our oldest ancestors clothed in animal skins. This image helps to match evolutionary thought for those who believe that the earliest humans were Neanderthals, cavemen. But you know that Adam and Eve were far beyond that mythical situation. So what would be the most valuable covering God could give humanity to cover his bare flesh?

Week 50, Day 4

...and clothed them.

Take time to look up the difference between flesh and skin. What does it say? The main difference between skin and flesh is that the skin is a soft outer covering organ of vertebrates, and flesh is a soft substance of an animal body that consists of muscle and fat. As you learned earlier, Adam and Eve had flesh but no skin. They are enclothed with light. But that covering was lost in their disobedience. So they covered themselves with what they had, leaves. God knew leaves would not be sufficient for living in a fallen world. So he gave them skin. The Hebrew words for light and skin are homonyms. They are spelled with one letter difference but sound the same when pronounced.

Week 50, Day 5

...garments of skin...

So God gives humanity skin. Take some time, and view Skin Facts. Look at the back of your hand. Touch and feel your skin. Now take a look at this article. Is that not amazing? God truly gave humanity a remarkable covering, allowing us to live in the earth's environment. When you jump in the pool, why do you close your mouth and maybe even hold your nose? So the water won't get in. But you never think about covering your body. Why? Because the skin doesn't leak. But it can absorb oxygen. God knew what man would need to exist apart from His presence, and He provided garments of skin.

Week 50, Day 6

...garments of skin...

For most people, skin and flesh are considered the same. But the Bible has always seen them as separate. Look at Leviticus 9:11. Now, look at a particular passage in Job 19:20-26. In verse 20, Job distinguishes between his skin and flesh. Then following a theologically significant passage concerning the Redeemer, Christ Jesus, Job shares a considerable truth. In verse 26, he says, "Even after my skin is destroyed, yet from my flesh, I shall see God." Skin is not necessary to be in the presence of God. There is one more passage for you to see, Ezekiel 37:6-8. It is the passage concerning the Valley of Dry Bones. When God brings back life to the dry bones, He makes flesh grow back, and then He covers them with skin.

Week 51, Day 1

Then the Lord God said, "Behold…

Behold is used to draw attention to the speaker. When you have invited a group for a meeting, you stand up and say, "Could I have your attention." Everyone in the room, who is listening, will turn and stare at you. But it also means drawing attention to something you have done. Twice in the first chapter of Genesis, the Lord uses the word behold. First, to draw attention to the provision, He has made for the Man. It is the second time to share that the creation is finished and good. But now we have just a little different form of the word. It is to draw attention, not for something the speaker has done, but for what others have done. It is an interjection of disappointment God is about to share with the others of the Trinity.

Week 51, Day 2

...the man has become like one of Us...

Read Genesis 3:5. The Serpent, Satan, says to the Woman, "you will be like God, knowing good and evil." Humanity was created in God's image, but until they ate of the tree of knowledge of good and evil, did they know good and evil? The statement the Serpent made was correct but was not good. Can you imagine giving the keys to your new car to a seven-year-old and telling them to take it out for a spin? If they made it out of the driveway, it wouldn't be long before the car would be wrecked. Why? Because a seven-year-old has not matured enough to handle driving a car. Suddenly Adam and Eve can make the same choices as God. They could determine good and evil. Yet, you have already seen they couldn't keep even the most straightforward command not to eat of the Tree of Knowledge of Good and Evil.

Week 51, Day 3

...and also take from the tree of life...

Take time to read Genesis 2:9. There were two particular trees that God caused to grow in Eden. The first was the tree of life. Nothing is said in Genesis concerning this tree until the third chapter. God reveals His concern that man, who has fallen due to sin, may well take and eat from the tree of life. What is the tree of life? Amazingly, the next place a physical tree of life is mentioned is at the end of the Bible in Revelation. John records in Revelation 2:7 that those that overcome the Lord will allow eating of the tree of life in the Paradise of God. You remember that the word Eden means paradise in Hebrew. The tree of life in Revelation is in the identical place as it was in Genesis, Paradise.

Week 51, Day 4

…and eat, and live forever…

Adam and Eve were designed and created by God to live forever in His presence. The tree of life is the doorway to that eternal presence. Revelation 22:14 says, "Blessed are those who wash their robes, so that they may have the right to the tree of life." What does it mean to wash their robes? Why do you wash your clothes? Because they are dirty. To clean them, you must wash them. When sin dirties your life, how do you make it clean? Confess and repent. That is what washing their robes means. Only those who confess Jesus as Lord and repent of their sin can take from the tree of life. Did Adam and Eve confess and repent? Sadly, the answer is NO.

Week 51, Day 5

…therefore the Lord God sent him out of the garden…

Proving the germ theory of disease was the crowning achievement of the French scientist Louis Pasteur. His view that microscopic organisms caused diseases was controversial in the 19th century. It opposed the accepted theory of "spontaneous generation." When you go to a hospital, the operating room is sterile and germ-free. There are countless procedures to remove all harmful microorganisms from the operating room. The same is true for the holiness of God. Sin cannot remain in the presence of the Lord. Adam and Eve had to leave the presence of God. Isn't it good to know that God has a place prepared for you that sin doesn't contaminate? "In My Father's house are many dwelling places; if it were not so, I would have told you; for I go to prepare a place for you. If I go and prepare a place for you, I will come again and receive you to Myself, that where I am, there you may be also." (John 14:2-3)

Week 51, Day 6

…to cultivate the ground from which he was taken.

All decisions lead to consequences. Sometimes those consequences lead to situations never imagined. In Genesis 1:28, Adam was given the authority to subdue the earth from which he was formed. God had even provided for his physical needs by having the land produce the necessary food. As a result of his sinful decision, he becomes not the ruler but the earth's servant. The very thing he was created to rule over now rules over him. This paradox is what sin does to all of humanity. When you choose to lie, you become the slave of the consequences of the lie. When you decide to steal, you become a slave to the consequences of the theft. Sinful choices never bring the freedom or the happiness you desire.

Week 52, Day 1

So He drove the man out...

If you had asked Adam, "Do you want to stay or go?" What do you think he would have said? The language of the verse tends to indicate that he wanted to stay in the garden. The guilt of sin doesn't force him to flee. He doesn't shamefully slink away into the night. The Bible says God had to drive him out of the garden. Despite humanity's sinful nature, all people desire to live in the presence of their Creator. Read Ecclesiastes 3:10-11. Solomon says that God has put eternity in the heart of every being. This desire to know God and be with Him motivates all humanity to attempt to create Eden in a fallen world. But Solomon also says that they will never be able to achieve their desire.

Week 52, Day 2

...He stationed the cherubim...

Clinical procedures for operating rooms state, "Sterile areas should be continuously kept in view. An unguarded sterile field is considered contaminated." The holiness of God demands the same attention. To that end, the Lord God stationed the cherubim at the entrance to Paradise. There can be no access to eternal life through the Tree of Life. Only when the genuinely holy One comes can the access be gained. Read Luke 23:39-43. What does Jesus say to the repentant thief on the cross? Read John 3:16. What does it say is available to those who believe in Jesus Christ? Even the cherubim (remember Satan is not in God's presence anymore) who dwell in the presence of God yield to the true King and His followers.

Week 52, Day 3

…to guard the way…

Read Matthew 7:13-14. What does Jesus say about "the way?" There are two ways or paths that a person can take in life. The first is broad, and it leads to destruction. The second is narrow and leads to life. He says the problem is that most people will take the broad way rather than the narrow. Why do you think that is true? The sinful nature of humanity makes the truth harder to find. Humanity's desire to be like God keeps them from seeing the way to the tree of life. What, then, is the way to the tree of life?

Week 52, Day 4

…to guard the way…

One of the great blessings of modern technology is Google Maps. When you want to go somewhere, you just put in the destination, and right away, you are given several options for travel. Each route will tell you the time it will take to reach your location. You also can choose in the options portion things such as avoiding tolls. Amazingly it can offer alternative routes to the same destination. It is easy to think that life is like a map: one destination but many ways to get there. But as you saw in Matthew, there is only one way to eternal life. Now read John 14:1-6. How does Jesus describe Himself in verse 6? "I am the way." There is only one way to reach the Tree of Life. It is by placing your faith in Jesus Christ.

Week 52, Day 5

...to the tree of life.

Ephesians 2:8 says, "For by grace you have been saved through faith; and that not of yourselves, it is the gift of God." God's gifts don't always seem gracious or kind. In the last passage of Genesis 3, God casts Adam and Eve from the garden. At first glance, it appears to be a negative judgment, but it is an act of grace in reality. If they had taken from the Tree of Life, they would have forced all humanity into eternal separation from God. They would have been permanently removed from God without any hope of avoiding the terrible consequences of sin. Yet God, in His great wisdom and grace, did not permit that to happen. More than that, He provided another tree that would restore the relationship humanity had lost.

Week 52, Day 6

... The tree of life.

Read about the most important tree in the history of the world in Galatians 3:13-14. Jesus said in John 3:14-15, "As Moses lifted up the serpent in the wilderness, even so must the Son of Man be lifted up; that whoever believes in Him will have eternal life." The authentic Tree of Life is the cross of Jesus Christ. On that tree, Christ paid the price for restoring your relationship with the God who created you. Through the curse of sin placed on Jesus, the penalty of sin was removed. You no longer have the consequences of sin but the eternal life God desired for humanity from the beginning of time.

www.ingramcontent.com/pod-product-compliance
Lightning Source LLC
Chambersburg PA
CBHW071000160426
43193CB00012B/1848